D1614543

Buckinghamshire Dialect

BUCKINGHAMSHIRE DIALECT

by

H. HARMAN

With a new Preface
by
STEWART F. SANDERSON,
Director, Institute of Dialect and Folk Life Studies,
University of Leeds.

Republished by S. R. Publishers Ltd., 1970

Originally Published by Hazell, Watson and Viney Ltd.,
London and Aylesbury
1929

1970. S.R. Publishers Ltd., East Ardsley, Wakefield, Yorkshire.

I.S.B.N. 0. 85409. 581. 0

Printed in England by Kingprint Limited.

PREFACE TO THE REPRINTED EDITION

Forty years have gone by since this book was first published. It has long been out of print; and since it has become something of a collector's piece for students of Buckinghamshire history, the proposal to reprint it is truly to be welcomed.

The County has seen many changes in these years, not least in respect of its population and patterns of settlement. New housing estates have grown up to accommodate over-spill—itself a new word—from London or to serve as dormitory suburbs in what today is know as the commuter belt. The old style of village life has altered radically, and so have the daily tasks, occupations and pastimes of farmer and ploughman, craftsman, labourer, shop-keeper and house-wife. These changes have naturally affected the subject-matter of the book—the spoken dialect of Buckinghamshire.

Our knowledge of English dialects and the ways in which we study them have also advanced, as have the technical resources available to the collector of dialect material. If one were to set out in the 1970's to compile a book on Buckinghamshire dialect, both the approach and the end-product would no doubt be different from Mr. Harman's; but that does not make his work any the less valuable in its historical context. The values have shifted, however. The interest of his book today lies less in its purely linguistic contribution and more in the picture it reflects of a passing way of life, which is mirrored both in the glossary and in the conversational sketches which he composed. Today one would tape-record actual conversations and trans-cribe them faithfully: they would have an authenticity as different in kind from Mr. Harman's sketches as genuine Chippendale furniture is different from reproductions. But the tape-recorder had not been invented; Ediphone machines were cumbersome and expensive; and Mr. Harman did the best he could with the means at his disposal. It is easy for the specialist to point to other shortcomings, and especially to the weakness of the book in terms of phonology. The orthographic conventions adopted by Harman were seen by his editor, G. Eland, to be far from satisfactory, though surprisingly enough he did not even remove such inconsistencies as using both *ge-aht* and *geeat* to represent the particular pronunciation of *gate* which Harman distinguished from another pronunciation *gai-aht*. Again, what is one to make of, for instance *mohur* for *motor*—is there a glottal stop or an aspirate or what? But once more we must remember that in Harman's day there were comparatively few trained phoneticians around to whom he could turn for advice and help in establishing spelling conventions or providing phonemic transcriptions in the alphabet of the International Phonetic Association.

If Harman was no philologist—he imperfectly understood the relationship between spelling and sound and was confused about the nature of the dipthong—he was nonetheless a good word-collector and phrase-collector, and had a keen ear for the style of the English speech he heard about him. The findings of the English Dialect Survey, which covered six localities in Buckinghamshire some thirty years later, confirm a number of points he made. To cite just a few examples from the *Survey of English Dialects* volumes, the plural form *housen* is confirmed at localities Bk 3 and 5; the pronunciations *thrail* and *frail* are found for *flail;* and the word *wanty* for the belly-band of a horse's harness is found at Bk 4, 5 and 6 in the east and south of the county. And there are further contributions which are not to be found in the *Survey of English Dialects,* either because they may have dropped out of use since Harman's day or because they escaped through the meshes of the

English Dialect Survey's net. Take for example the word *geely-balk* for the iron bar from which the pot-hook is hung in an old-fashioned fireplace: the *Survey of English Dialects* has found the word in Lincolnshire and Norfolk but not as far south as Buckinghamshire, and Joseph Wright's *English Dialect Dictionary* (1898) does not report the word from Buckinghamshire either. Another example is *hatchel*, hay raked up into a row: the *Survey of English Dialects* has not encountered the word, while the *English Dialect Dictionary* knows it in Northamptonshire and Sussex only. In the field of syntax and grammar there are also interesting contributions: while it is true that Harman's conversation-pieces are his own compositions, one is surely justified in trusting his reportage of proverbial phrases and expressions, and of such remarks as 'I shull say as the gal said when she had hur chap to tay fur the fust time: "Chap ur no chap, sahcer mi tay I ull, fur burn mi chops I unt." '

More important still, however, is the range of material illuminating the folk life of rural Buckinghamshire half-a-century ago and more—one of Harman's informants recounted memories which went back as far as the 1850's. In the conversation–pieces, incidentally, there is no romantic nonsense about the good old times. 'If they waunt em, let em have em!' said one stalwart who went to work as a boy for a shilling a week at a period when a horseman's wage was eight shillings. This certainly strikes an authentic note in the scale of social attitudes.

Memories of feasts and fairs, of mummers, and of traditional meat and drink are enshrined in these pages along with the text of a folksong, stories of ghosts and hauntings, and accounts of the seasons for planting various crops, threshing corn with a flail, hay-making, and the building of a witchert wall.

One would welcome more compilations of this kind from every part of England, to preserve the record of the past in the language of the countryman.

STEWART F. SANDERSON
Director,
Institute of Dialect and Folk Life Studies,
University of Leeds.
December 1969.

EDITOR'S PREFACE

IN the ordinary way it is a far easier task for an editor than for an author to write a preface. The poor author has to rake up the threadbare excuses of a "long-felt want," a wish to amuse or instruct, or the importunity of friends; so long as he keeps in the background his true intent, which is to impress the world with his knowledge, it scarcely matters what he says.

In this particular case, when small fame and no pecuniary reward are in prospect, our Author may be believed when he tells us that he has recorded words and conversations merely because they are rapidly falling into disuse. He has tried to capture a local usage before it becomes a mere echo; he has made his *apologia*, however, and it remains for the Editor to attempt a justification of his own intervention.

This is not altogether easy, but at least the extent of his responsibility must be made clear in justice to Mr. Harman.

The collection interested him because nothing has hitherto been attempted in the way of a serious collection of Bucks dialect. The only printed record known to the English Dialect Society [1] was a very poor article which appeared in *Good Words* [2] and was quoted in *The Times*. [3] Since those days some vocabularies have appeared in the *Records of Bucks*, [4]

---

[1] In their list of works dealing with Dialects printed in 1877.
[2] July 1869.　　　　　　　　　[3] 12 July 1869.
[4] Vol. vii, pp. 61–70 and 284–303, and vol. ix, pp. 124–72.

and other places, but nothing in the way of an attempt to print complete dialogue has been made.

It was Mr. Harman's intention to give a somewhat scientific account of the sounds and to indicate their possible origin, but without a complete training in phonetics he hesitated to plunge into the stormy seas, where Philology plays the part of Scylla and Phonology that of Charybdis. To have done this would have been taking risks against which nothing but expert seamanship could prevail; Mr. Harman's modesty led him to consider himself unqualified for the test, and his Editor is grateful, recalling how one grammarian cried to another, "God confound you for your theory of impersonal verbs!"[1]

The intention beneath the following pages therefore is to present the actual speech of Buckinghamshire, without drawing any deductions or offering any theories. It is a mere attempt to preserve some local words and usages before they are swept away by the tide of a nationally standard speech, or before all memory of the thing or the action connoted by the word perishes. As Horace says: *Verborum vetus interit aetas,* and a living language, like a living organism, must adapt itself to the changing environment of new times and customs.

For the Glossary at the end the Editor accepts responsibility; it could have been greatly extended, but words imported were omitted on the one hand, and those in general dialectal use on the other.

The artless and almost insipid character of the conversations is the best proof that they are un-

[1] Isaac D'Israeli's *Curiosities of Literature,* article upon Literary Controversy."

sophisticated; their matter-of-fact tone is evidence of their authenticity. Association of place or subject may make one or another conversation the reader's favourite, but attention is drawn to two of very different types, each most admirably handled. The first is at Drayton Parslow (p. 52) and contains a ghost set in a good narrative; the second is of considerable importance from a sociological point of view. This is Mr. Plastow's account of the Inclosure at Haddenham (p. 93); this is a definite addition to our knowledge, but the whole conversation makes a truly " human document."

Were not Mr. Harman truly modest he might say in earnest as the great Dean said ironically in the Introduction to his *Polite Conversation*:

"If my favourable and gentle Readers would consider with what attention I listened to all Discourses, the better to retain them in my Memory, and then at proper Seasons withdrew unobserved, to enter them in my Table-book, while the Company little suspected what a noble Work I had then in Embrio; I say, if all this were known to the World, I think it would be no great Presumption in me to expect the publick Thanks of both Houses of Parliament for the Service and Honour I have done to the whole Nation by my Single Pen."

G. ELAND.

TABLE OF CONTENTS

TABLE OF CONTENTS

INTRODUCTION

IN the early days of the Board Schools, about 1880, I was standing upon West Wycombe Hill with a school-fellow, and he asked me how it was that the boys from Wheeler End who attended our school always halved their vowels? Although this was not expressed quite correctly, I knew the peculiarity of speech to which he referred, so I agreed that I had noticed the same practice among all those who lived in the neighbouring hamlets. He quoted as instances *tai-ahk* for "take," *mai-ahd* for "made," *che-ahr* for "chair," *ge-aht* for "gate," *sai-ahm* for "same," and *lai-ahn* for "lane." The discussion went no further at that time, as our attention was drawn to other topics, but the sudden directness of the question made it recur to my memory for long afterwards.

Soon after this incident we were attending the Sunday afternoon service at the little chapel; this was in the days when three services were taken each Sunday. The preacher was an old shepherd who lived not far from Bledlow Ridge ("Bledlur," the old inhabitants pronounce it), and his lesson was from the fourth chapter of the Book of Daniel, in which is told the awful punishment meted out to Nebuchadnezzar for his overweening pride when viewing the great city of Babylon. He gave a very intelligent rendering of the piece, and this, combined with the quaintness of his speech, attracted the attention of his youthful congregation, who had received the benefit of five or six years' Board School education. There had been some signs of levity as the

chapter proceeded, but unrestrained signs of amuse-
ment quite out of place with the spirit in which the
Service was conducted broke out when the climax
of Nebuchadnezzar's doom was expressed in the
following terms:

> "Till his he-ahrs were grown like e-ahgle's
> fedders, an his ne-ahls like bird's claas."

These instances of the vernacular have been taken
from two villages which are admittedly situated near
together, and it might be thought that this form of
speech was a local growth, the result of isolation and
detachment from the culture of the more populous
centres of the county. The old communal and clan
spirit lasted quite up to the "fifties"; most villages
were complete communities in themselves, every
trade necessary to meet the wants of the inhabitants
and the outlying farms was in operation to supply
the wants of life and the occupational demands of
the district. There was but little necessity to visit
the towns, and wages were partly paid in kind. Thus
the village was the centre of parish life and very little
intercourse was held with its neighbours.

This state of affairs, together with the lack of
mechanical transport, almost complete absorption in
agriculture, and the absence of organised education,
combined to perpetuate old customs and old forms
of speech; and there is not the least doubt that some
of these sounds and constructions are survivals of a
former age, passing down the centuries unaffected
by outside influences, and still preserving English as
pure as the approved standard of modern speech.

The effect of these survivals upon one unaccustomed to them may be illustrated by an incident which took place at Quainton about 1878. A schoolmistress from the London district took up her duties and was really puzzled to understand the scholars' conversation and requests, a common one being: "Plee-ahs, miss, I ant got nair a sle-aht." These doubled vowel-sounds, which are much used there at the present day, were unintelligible to her. One morning a little girl had committed some slight misdemeanour and was punished by detention. When the time came for her to go, the mistress said to her, "You may go home," but the child did not move. She repeated it more emphatically, but still the child made no attempt to move. One of the assistant teachers, who realised the position and afterwards told me the incident, then went to the girl and said, "Goo-an hoo-am!" The child immediately rose and left the school.

Not only is this form of speech general in the central and western parts of the county, but there is no difference between Waddesdon and Wheeler End, Quainton and Gawcott, Preston Bissett and Pitstone, nor between any other places where the dialect is used.

To demonstrate this, some examples are given:

Quainton, 1924:
   "I be a seeaving mi money fur Aiuhlsburry feear."

Gawcott, 1925:
   (1) Woodman, when asked if there are snakes there, replies: "Plenty a sneeaks."

(2) The customer of an inn upon being brought cloudy ale says: "Taiak this back; tis too thick."

(3) The secretary of the cricket club asks: "Tom, ull ye maiak one a the teeam tomorra night?" Another player asks: "Wheeur do ye play?" and receives the answer: "At Buckinghum; tis a jolly good pleeace to play crickut; we alwiz have a good gaiam theeur."

(4) "He an't got his waiastcooat an this arternoon."

(5) Said to unruly boys in chapel: "I ull a paice."

(6) "When he come to mi house he'd ony got his thin slippurs an, an if he'd a said anything else I'd a jumped acrass his fitt and he'd ad some smoshed uns. If that ant a done him, I'd a fotch the black stick down and fot him to the ground."

(7) "The waiker we git the cleverer we git."

(8) Theeur allus was a harvist and theeur allus ull be."

Tingewick, 1925:

(1) "My son went to Acton, wheeur he larnt beeakerin."

(2) "I was asked to treeace the coourse a the spring; so I went zigzag acrass the meddur, which was about foour aiacres, and put down the pegs behind me. When I'd finished they were as streeat as a line."

The man of Bucks, like other Englishmen, dislikes to make himself conspicuous, so that when a farmer's son finds himself in the company of those who speak the Received Standard English, he conforms to the best of his ability; but amongst his friends he uses the old forms with a freedom and facility which are the heritage of generations who have done the same. This diffidence applies in particular to the south of the county. In the company of typical country-men I have always found, during the first few evenings, that they exercised a certain restraint upon their expressions, and it was only when good-fellowship prevailed and confidence obtained that their native speech returned.

At Steeple Claydon once I visited an inn much frequented by the inhabitants. When I entered, the room was full of typical Bucks labourers, and I sat in the corner and listened. Directly a hush fell on the company, and all that I could get was: "That's the new schooulmaster," and the conversation whilst I was present was as near the ordinary standard as one could expect. When I left I had no doubt that the homely old tongue was in full swing. On other occasions I have heard an old dialectal speaker correct himself in the characteristic sounds and utter them in a more conventional way when amongst strangers. Whilst visiting Turweston last summer I met an old inhabitant at the beginning of the village, so I said: "Is this Turston?" "No," said he; "this is Tur-weston." Later a roadman at Worminghall corrected me when I spoke of the parish as "Wurnall." [1]

[1] J. Tanner: *History of Worminghall*, p. 8, says: "Colloquially speaking it is more often Wornall than Worminghall." This was in 1884; H. Lupton, in his *History of Thame*, 1860, p. 1, calls it "Wornall" and nothing else.

This inclination for correct expression pervades the county throughout its length and breadth, and in the end can only result in suppressing the more extreme forms which give such a characteristic charm; at the same time the less noticeable may escape and survive for many years to come.

The unrounding of the *o*, the abbreviation of "have" to *a*, and the raising of *e* to *i* in certain constructions seem to increase, not only in the villages but in the industrial centres, to such an extent that they have become universal throughout the county among the native artisan and labouring population.

I left the Downley Board School in 1887 at the termination of my apprenticeship, and during that time I was fully conversant with the dialectal usages of the district west of High Wycombe. The broader features at that time were still well preserved in the surrounding hamlets and villages, but they were not so prominent in West Wycombe. Many came from the Commons to work in North's factory, and many passed on their way to market every Friday, so that I had more than a casual association with many of these people whose dialect was so frequent that it called for no comment on the part of any resident in the village. The speakers were generally of fairly advanced age and had escaped the influence of the School Board Act of 1870.

On my return to Bucks in 1918 I found that most of the old faces were gone, and in the place of their old homely speech there was the drab and colourless substitute which had been fashioned by five decades of classroom teaching. Instead of these old fellows with their jolly, round, ruddy faces, their hearty greetings and generous impulses, there was the pallor of the machine-shop and the factory.

So seldom did I hear the old broad tongue that I began to think our dialect had almost died out, as wherever I went there seemed to be not the slightest vestige left. However, in 1923 I was sent to Waddesdon, and while there I mentioned the matter to two of my colleagues, one a native of the village and the other of Brill. They assured me that I was entirely wrong as regards the places they lived in, and that the old forms of speech were as usual amongst workers on the land as at any time in their recollection.

One afternoon, towards the end of the gardening lesson, I naïvely asked a boy how the old people pronounced the word "spade." He immediately replied, "Speead," and proceeded to give other examples. Soon after, when the order to return to school had been given, I heard: "Cam an! bring that thaiur speead. Dooant furgit the fark. Whosen's reeak's this? Open the geeat." At last I had, regretfully, to suppress the talk. Now that the ice was broken, many of the boys were anxious to give their quota, repeating what they had heard in the village. Many of the sayings came from a dialectal speaker now dead, and I give a few. The first is a typical example of rustic philosophy:

(1) "If ye a got a grudge agen anybody, gi him a peear a ood pidgins; they ull ett a peck a carn a day."

(2) A train being delayed at a station, the speaker puts his head out of the window and says: "Master, if ye dooant set the treean an, I shull git out and walk."

7

(3) Father to son: "You larn too much nowa-deeas, my boey."

From what I heard, it was clear that the old sounds still persisted among the children, and I determined to test a few of the older scholars. It was near Christmas and there was the old spirit in the atmosphere of the school which was anticipating the greatest of our Christian festivals. The children were jubilant, as all examinations were finished, the lists up, positions in class decided, and the monotony of lessons was over for a few weeks. Hymns and carols were sung with gusto to the old tunes, and all were touched with that joyous abandon which I hope will never be suppressed or eradicated from our elementary schools at this time. The day before leaving I asked some of the older scholars to write for me a composition in the old Bucks language on any subject they pleased. Their compositions were a revelation and examples from them will be given at the close of this book. And here I should like to warn any who might, in a captious spirit, say: "This is the result of our modern education! See what they are taught in schools!" I can truthfully say that these compositions were made by scholars who, in their ordinary work, were equal to any in accuracy of grammar, originality of expression, and fullness of description.

This was not my only experience in this way, for in many places to the north and west of Aylesbury I have ascertained that the old forms are well known to the children, who never attempt to use them when on the school premises. This proved that I must modify considerably the idea I had formed that the dialect was almost a thing of the past. Once whilst lodging at the house of an old native of Nash, who then lived at Stony Stratford, I was told of a girl of seven who accompanied her mother on a visit to her old home. The girl's aunt had received no warning of the visit, and said as she laid the tea-table, "I ant got any keeak fur tay, as I dint know ye were acomin." Throughout the visit she continued to speak the old tongue, which her sister, the child's mother, used herself in her early days. The next day, when home again and about to start for school, she said to her mother, "I haiat gooin to schooul," showing how easily the use of dialect comes to one predisposed but not used to it.

A little later the child's grandfather came to visit his daughter at Stony Stratford. The fashion of bobbing hair had only just been introduced, and seeing one who had undergone the process, the old man exclaimed, "Poour thing! what a sheeam!"

At Drayton Parslow once I entered the post office and found already there two little girls, of whom one was a bright, merry child of seven, exceptionally forward in her lessons, very fluent in her reading, and responsive to any question which might be put to her; her usual pronunciation had no trace of dialectal influence. The postmistress asked the girl for the money.

LITTLE GIRL: "E gin it ye. E put half a crown an the teeable."

POSTMISTRESS: "Where did you put it?"

LITTLE GIRL: "Jest heeur."

POSTMISTRESS: "Well, it isn't there."

LITTLE GIRL: "E knows e did. E knows e put it an the teeable."

Whilst this conversation went on I had. been writing on a postcard; feeling some irregularity in the surface of the card, I lifted it and found the half-crown. "Here it is," I said. "There, e knowed e put it an the teeable," said the little girl.

This split-vowel sound is now rarely met with in school and playground. I have listened carefully to the ordinary conversation of our scholars and marked hundreds, perhaps thousands, of composition exercises, and only once did I find a boy, from Dodder-shall, writing "*fiar*" for "fair"; this was more than clerical metathesis, as he would speak of "Aiuhlsburry feear."

Although these forms are absent, one must not suppose that the children's talk is free from dialect; the following specimen was taken down at Stoken-church during January 1926, at the beginning of the "marble season." I stood by the side of some nine or ten merry little fellows during one play-time, when they were playing at "tipping," and noted the following exclamations:

"Tip me fuur, Poker. Cam an then. Six in. Got em. Now then, what be ye up to? Git out a the way. Five in. They be mine. Tip me six. Seven in. They be yourn. If I daunt win I shant play agen. Tip me six. I shant; tip somebody else. Now then, Smiler, I ull tip ye eight. That's too much. Tip me six. Cam an. I daunt want to tip eight. I ull tip the lot an em. Three in. Yourn, Smiler. Tip me a dozen. Ant got em.

Tip me fuur then. Pick em up. We ant got time to wait about. Tip me eight, Poker. I wunt; I ull tip ye fuur. Five in. I be bummuxed; [1] britch me up. Heeur's a couple. Tip me two. Three in. Bummuxed agen. Cam an. One in. I a lost. Out a th' way. Git an. I know e be. I a bin and won two. Six in. Goo an. Whoo's a gooin to a a game in the ring? Hi! hi! hi! I be good at marbles! Tip me fuur. Gaw, cam an out a the way. Tip somebody. Buck up; the bell ull soon ring. Five in. Goo an, Bill.

Having noted these exclamations from children at their games, I determined at the first opportunity to obtain specimens of the conversation of the adults, and to effect this I visited one or two old inns where I thought a representative company of the villagers would be assembled. I was not very successful for a few nights, as amongst those with whom I passed a few evenings were many who worked in Wycombe, and this one circumstance militated against the retention of the old forms. However, one very dark night, I stood on the path by the Water Tower and debated with myself as to where to pass the evening, when my eyes were attracted by the bright lights of an inn situated on the far side of the common. I decided to go over and chance my luck.

Picking my way through the deep cart ruts and by the side of many timber logs stacked for sawing, I reached the Flower-de-Luce (Fleur-de-Lys) and went

[1] This word is not apparently given by Wright; it is known in the Vale as well as on the hills, and seems to mean " cleared out."

in. I entered the taproom, and, as was my wont, sat quietly down in a corner next the door, picked up a paper, and commenced to read. The room was beautifully warm, for on the opposite side of the door blazed the finest fire that I had ever seen in my travels throughout Bucks. In the wide, old-fashioned fireplace stood an iron framework on a raised platform exactly under a wide canopy of brickwork which had been built in the mouth of the chimney, and through which the smoke ascended. Some fifteen or sixteen boughs, each about a yard long, lay across the framework, and were burning fiercely and brightly; at the same time they were filling the room with the delightful fragrance that comes from no other wood but our native beech. The heat pervaded the room and sent a comfort throughout which was delightful to experience. In the corner by the fireplace sat an old man, smoking his clay, and on the same side were other old inhabitants. On the opposite side was a group playing dominoes, and by their exclamations I realised I was in a company whose vernacular was little changed by modern influences.

A night or two afterwards, I commenced to enter into the conversation. "A fine fire," I said to the landlord. "Ah," he replied, "the Fleur-de-Lys has allus been noted for its fires." At the same time the domino players had not the usual quota for the game, so the time was spent in casual talk, during which the old gentleman referred to said, when discussing the merits of shove-halfpenny, "Ole Chawley Johnson could alwiz tell what ai-ahpenny he got by the fee-ul an it." On another subject one remarked, "He got his ai-apron an when he was a-carrin the pleeats." Soon one of the company departed and left the door open. "Shet that dur-ur," shouted the old gentleman. "When anybody goos out they alwiz leeav the du-ur open an nivver think a shettin it; the draught's enough to blow anybody away." One of the players then said to me: "Ull ye maiak one fur a gaiam a dominoes?" "Thank you," said I; "I am not much of a player." "Well," he said, "we want one moo-ur to maiak the fu-ur." "Heeur's White," says another when the door opened; "he ull maiak one." "Ull ye plai-ah [play], White?" "Yis," replied the latter; "I ull!"

The following remarks on the game were then noted: "Shull we draa fur partners? We nivver do a much luck when we plai-ah togither. No, we nivver do. Anywee-ahs, we ull see what we can do to-night. We shull a to cheeange saits. Now then, shufful em! Draa! Goo-an! I ull start wi a three. Good! Ai-aht! I knowed ye had it. A good gaiam! Shufful! Very well plai-ahd! Keep an! How do we stand? A purty three! A purty three! Come along! Thaiur's another ai-ahpenny gone! Got em? How do we stand? Ye be in front. How many moour to git? Seven! A gurt one! A gurt one! A gurt one! Anywee-ahs, I ull plai-ah two; a double one, I mean! Purty! Purty! Purty. I a maiad a mistaiak! I maiad a mistaiak. I a——. If e had a plai-ahd the fu-ur, e should a got em! Draa! Yu-ur turn. Goo-an! Good aivening, Chawley! How is it outside? A ree-anin jest a little! Come along! A good gaiam. A very good gaiam. Three times e a plai-ahd an ony got one aich time. A one moour! Shufful! Draa! Now then! Goo-an!

Ha! ha! ha! I know wheeur he is! E shant plai-ah what ye want! Tha's a good un. Tha's a good un! Keep an! Five an three maiaks ai-aht! Nair a one! A gurt one! How do the gaiam stand? Five wanted. Ai-aht an one fur domino maiaks nine! Tha's done it!"

For the past ten years I have travelled throughout the length and breadth of Bucks, and during this period I have had more ample opportunities than fall to the lot of most residents to note the state of our dialect as it is at the present time. Owing to my duties, I have been brought into intimate contact with the people who, in face of the influences of modern times, have preserved the old methods of speech. Fifty or sixty years ago the task of collecting a detailed account of these forms would have been easy in comparison with what it has been during the past decade. Then most of our villagers could speak no other than the homely tongue which they had inherited from their forefathers; now, from my own observation and from reports of other people, there are few indeed who can speak none but their county dialect.

Many influences have combined to bring this about. First is the very powerful one produced by the laying down of land to grass, with the resultant displacement of the original labourers from the villages and their removal to other forms of toil, chiefly factory work. Taking Gawcott as an example, there are at present only four men and two boys employed on the five farms in the village; thirty years ago there were at least twenty men and a corresponding number of boys.

Another great influence is the effect of our present standardised education during the most impressionable period of life.

There is also the self-consciousness of people who feel, in the company of others observing a received standard of speech, that they must conform so far as they can with conventional usage and repress their own dialectal tendencies.

So far as these pages are concerned, the district to the south and east of High Wycombe is of no importance; settlement by "foreigners" has effectively obliterated dialect. In places like Slough, Datchet, Langley, Stoke Poges, Wraysbury, and Iver I have found the speech just as one finds it in a London suburb. On the ridges to the west of High Wycombe, like Naphill, Booker, Wheeler End, and Lane End, and further on at Lacey Green and Bledlow Ridge, many traces survive among the older people; forty years ago these places were strongly dialectal.

Even at Turville, situate as it is at the edge of the woods and far removed from any busy roads, I found the conversation principally about High Wycombe, Downley Pitch, and Bradenham; it showed no trace of the old sounds, the influence of the Wycombe valley was marked, and I came away with nothing. Later I found that an omnibus every day took a number of workmen from Fingest and Skirmett to and from High Wycombe, and the environment of the Wycombe chair factories reacted upon Hambleden, Turville, and Fingest—villages as remote as any in the county. When a district like this is subject to such influences it is no wonder that our old vernacular is rare to the east of Aylesbury;

on the west it is far more strongly pronounced.
Indeed, one can vouch that in the part of the county
to the west of Aylesbury and excluding the extreme
north, there are in almost every village people who
habitually speak dialect.

Stokenchurch, Drayton Parslow, and Gawcott are
the three villages with which I am familiar where
the dialect is most often heard. At Gawcott, in
particular, the old vernacular is so prevalent in
ordinary conversation that it is doubtful whether
there is a single person in the village unacquainted
with it. Until recent renovations took place, the
New Inn at Gawcott was an excellent example of
a late seventeenth- or early eighteenth-century house,
with a steep, thatched roof to give it dignity outside,
and within was a large settle which was the regular
evening meeting-place of the older inhabitants. All
had been on the land and their interest in it had never
waned. Their conversation, especially on some local
topic, was strongly dialectal.

It is from old associations like these in many parts
of the county that the materials of this book have
been collected; should it fall into hands where some
conversation may be recognised, it must be stated
clearly that it has been recorded in no spirit of levity,
but with deep gratitude for the privilege and good
fortune accorded to me in hearing our old Bucks
speech, for which I have had a deep and affectionate
regard all my life.

CHARACTERISTICS OF THE BUCKS DIALECT

IT is proposed to give illustrations of some of the points which most strike the listener to a Bucks dialect-speaker. Apart from technical and archaic words, which are given in the Glossary at the end of the book, there are particular sounds and usages of words which may be found all over the less sophisticated parts of the county.

These general conclusions have been grouped as follows:

I. Vowel Sounds.
II. Letters Dropped or Reversed.
III. Pronouns.
IV. Verbs.
V. Plural in -en.

After these general summaries, examples of actual conversations are given, arranged in alphabetical order of place-names.

The idea of a phonetic representation of sounds has been dropped, and it only remains to make such use of the ordinary alphabet as may convey some notion of the sound to those who have ever heard it. The vowel *a* generally has the value *ah*, though not when it is substituted for *o* or *e*, thus the preposition *on* will often [1] be spelled *an,* the pronunciation being *ann*.

[1] This word illustrates the difficulty of an inexpert editor; thus Mr. Harman sometimes writes "awfin," and "awf" for *often* and *off.* The Oxford English Dictionary supports the practice of the "best people" in giving "awfn" and "awf" as perfectly correct pronunciations of the respective words. In one place Mr. Harman gives us "Bister," but no other pronunciation is ever used for *Bicester*. Finally it has been decided to leave the spelling as recorded.—EDITOR.

Sometimes the consonant following the vowel is doubled to assist the sound. The expert will certainly be dissatisfied, but it is hoped that the general reader will not be unduly irritated.

I. Vowel Sounds

Professors Mawer and Stenton, in their Introductory Remarks to *The Place-names of Buckinghamshire*,[1] say: "One fact is clear, that Buckinghamshire in its early days was definitely not an *i* county." They had place-names in mind, but there is evidence to support it in the dialect. It is true that on the eastern side of the county, as far down as West Wycombe, we find *sich* for "such"; *jest* or *jist* for "just"; and *shet* for "shut." On the other hand, we have a very widely spread "u" sound in final unaccented syllables, where Received Standard English has "i" or "e." Thus we always hear: *rabbut, buckut, turnup, tickut, markut, sockut*, etc. *Trustles* for "trestles"—at Haddenham; and *purished* for "perished" in various places. *Thurn* for "thorn" is heard in places so widely scattered as Drayton Parslow, Haddenham, and Datchet.

That this is no modern phase, but the remains of a very old sound, is proved by a letter from Peter Caversham, who was Abbot of Notley in our county from 1480 to 1503. Writing [2] to Sir William Stonor soon after his election, he uses the phrases "such a sympull writer as I am," "trobull hym," and "an hondur pond." This clearly indicates that the "u"

---

[1] P. xxv.

[2] *The Stonor Letters and Papers,* ed. by C. L. Kingsford, vol. ii, p. 136.

sound was customary with so cultured a person as an Abbot at the close of the fifteenth century.

Then we also have "far" pronounced *fur* all over the county. *Purty* and *prutty* are usual for "pretty," and the second form is often abbreviated, especially in the Wycombe district, in such a phrase as "prut nigh."

At Waddesdon in 1924 I gave Andrew Marvell's "Song of the Emigrants in Burmudas" to the upper-standard boys to commit to memory. After an interval of time in which to learn it, I tested the scholars one afternoon. The second boy, who was a bright and able lad, gave the 25th and 26th lines thus:

> With cedars *chusen* by his hand
> From Lebanon he stores the land.

My attention was immediately drawn to the word *chusen*, so when he had finished, I told him to repeat it and be careful. He did so, and again said "chusen." I pointed out to him that the word should be "chosen," not "chusen," but had for reply, "Sir, I always say it, and I have heard other people do the same."

Another characteristic of Bucks speech is the practice of splitting a diphthong, or of interpolating an additional vowel-sound, and it will be found that words so treated adopt two forms themselves, thus we find:

Mare	.	.	*me-ahr*	and	*mai-ahr*
Cheap	.	.	*che-ahp*	,,	*chai-ahp*
Bean	.	.	*be-ahn*	,,	*bai-ahn*
Gate	.	.	*ge-aht*	,,	*gai-aht*

In many places there is a decided tendency not only to split the diphthong, but to lower the final sound to "u," giving us:

beeust for *beast*
feeust „ *feast*
cheeur „ *chair*

The numerals "four" and "fourteen" and the possessive adjective "your" almost invariably are broken up into *fu-ur, fu-urteen,* and *yu-ur.* At Stokenchurch in 1926 this was very pronounced during the daily calling of the registers, the children declaring their attendance by numbers. On every occasion one heard *fu-ur,* and *fu-urteen,* even if a repetition were called for.

In some villages there is a tendency to use *fow-er* for "four," and they could certainly claim precedence for this at Middle Claydon, whence in 1656 William Roades, Sir Ralph's trusty steward, wrote [1] in a letter to Dr. Denton: "near worth fower score pound."

One commonly hears the sounds *uv* for "of," *ur* for "or," *nur* for "nor," *fur* for "for," *frum* for "from," *befu-ur* for "before," and *nuther* for "neither."

On the other hand, the diphthong in "brook" is often heard shortened to *bruck.* At Aston Abbotts I heard said jokingly, "Come an have a drap a Rowsham Bruck."

Occasionally "e" becomes short *a,* as the following specimens prove:

---

[1] *Verney Memoirs,* 1894, vol. iii, p. 274.

Drayton Parslow, 1926:

TEACHER. "What do you intend to do this afternoon?"

BOY. "I shall *adge* the path, sir."

Gawcott:

"Why, that chap he has to help him *slaips* by the side a the troughs and nivver hurts. They bring *mait* from all parts, even from Aiuhlsburry, any ole horse or cow as a died, and he gies a good price for 't. He coont git any tuther *waik,* so he was a bit upset how to *faid* the flies."

Stokenchurch, 1926:

Composition by Standard VI scholar: "We took our tea down in the meadows, and when we had finished it we played games for the rest of the evening. Everything went a *trait.*"

In a composition by a boy in Standard VI at Stokenchurch there appeared to be a preference for "e" instead of "a":

"And the hares set on their hind legs and listened."

The following examples illustrate some of the points mentioned above:

Aylesbury Station (January 1926):

PORTER. "You come down an the Great Western an you ull a to go back an it. If you goo back an tuther line, they ull charge you at Baker Street."

Gawcott, 1925:

A. "Good aivenin, mahster, how be ye a gittin an?"

B. "Pritty well, Will. How be you?"

A. "About as usual; bin hard at it to-day carrin. We a neeurly finished now. Ant got much more to do. We a got it up in pritty good order, an that's a good thing. I a jest come from the yard and I a had my little nephew down wi me; cant kaip him away, he ull come down an see what I be doin. He ain't affeard a the horses; they a got quite used to him and they follur him about. Ony tuther day they follured him down to the geeat; they were two old meears, treeace horses, and nivver attempted to step an him. Do you know him, mahster? He's in the Infants'; he's about seven now."

B. "Yes, I know him."

A. "Tuther Sunday he come to dinnur and he allus likes to sit an mi knee at the teeable when we be having it. We had got three pidgins as mi mahster had shot, we frit em up out a the yard, and as they flew round he brought down three and gin em me. Some people doant like em; I do, ispecially when they be baiaked in the ovun. He was sittin an his cheear and when they were put an the teeable he comes round and sits an mi knee. I put one an mi pleeat and as soon as I laid it down he started an it, and picked all the mait from the breast and part a the legs. Youngsturs allus like other people's food bettur nor their oo-an. Well, he stuck thaiur till we had finished. I very often taiak him for a ride. We were gooin to Buckinghum one Sahurday a few waiks agoo, an when we gets to the pitch as leeads down into the town, he says: 'Uncle, maiak em gallup, you made em gallup uphill, now maiak em gallup downhill.' Ah, mahster, that woont a done; but I was obliged to laugh at him. He's a fine little fellur."

Tingewick, 1925:

A. "Well, mahster, I a found ye a cheean" (*chain*).

B. "Wheeur did ye find it?"

A. "In the ditch."

B. "That's jest like my men; leeav things about anywheeur. Wheeur is it?"

A. "In the house. I a took ceeare an it fur twelve months."

B. "Goo and fetch it and ye can have a pint."

Drayton Parslow, 1926:

A. "Now then, I ull answer any question on agriculture anybody's likely to ask. I ull tell ye what 't is, we want good workmen an the land—men as ull work fur ther mahsters and so git a little carn fur therselves ivvery wik."

SMALLHOLDER. "And ivvery day, I suppooas?"

A. "Yis: ivvery day by wurkin ovurtime. You cant put old heads an young shelders. We a got some good old uns, but the young uns wunt be told. They know bettur than anybody else. I see a young fellur tuther day layin a hedge, but he was doin it wrong, and it woont a done to a told him. We want men as ull be told and wurk for ther mahsters, an they ull git some carn for therselves."

SMALLHOLDER. "An precious little an it, too."

A. "I'm heeur to answer any questions an agriculture."

SMALLHOLDER. "Well, I'll ax ye one: how many ai-acres do you cultiva-at?"

A. "That dooant matter. I pay mi men as much as anybody else."

In January 1928, at Gawcott, a pronounced dialectal speaker described another person, not present, as "a buzzy little man." This pronunciation was formerly common, but is now seldom heard. I was able to confirm this sound, however, by learning that there was a man in the neighbourhood who, from his active habits, was always called "Buzzy Bennett."

Preston Bissett:

A. "Hullo! wheeur be ye a-gooin?"

B. "I beeant a-gooin anywheeur."

A. "That ye be!"

B. "No, I beeant; I be a-gooin back."

Another native of Preston Bissett on a very dark night cried:

"Keeat, Keeat, I cant find the geeat. Come out and taiak the paiaper!"

Aston Abbotts, 1926:

"I was nivver in sich a storm as I were about two yeeurs agoo. I was a-wurkin in that feeuld tuther side a Wing rooad and I could see it a-comin. I put my cooat an and got under some trees by the side a the rooad and it very sun druv me out. The reean come down in torrents and went right through my cooat and I was wet to the skin."

Gawcott, 1925:

OLD WOMAN (to man teasing her cat). "I like

24

my cat as much as you like yuur dog. Let her alooan!"

Lane End, 1926:
"Her hand feels jest like a tooad's when ye ketch hold an it."

Wheeler End (County Council Election, 1923):
"Why dooant ye vooat fur yur own maiat?"

West Wycombe:
"How much more a ye got to pick up?"
"About two moour looad."

Bledlow Ridge:
"Ole Chummy had been down to college at Aiuhlsburry three months and they'd nearly killed him. Soon arter he come out he went down the laian wi some moour fellurs one mornin, an they see an ole heear at fu-urm jest over th' hedge. So one says, 'Chummy, goo and fetch yur gun.' 'No,' says Chummy, 'I a got to a six months next time.' Howivver he went and got it. One an em poked the gun through th' hedge and shot the heear dead; it nivver muv, so another run over and got it. As he was gooin to git it, a kaiper come out a the laian furder down and cheeased em right up into the village. Howivver, by the time he got theear, both the heear and the gun were in a saiaf pleeace and nobody was to be sin."

Drayton Parslow, 1926:
A. "I see the floods were out at Hardick this mornin."

B. "That wer the pleeace I was neeurly killed at some yeeurs ago. Some five or six an us were comin home from Aiuhlsburry reeaces one moonlight night and jest as we got to the bridge some ole ducks stood up in the water and flapped ther wings. Our hoss went like mad up the hi-ull to Wichurch; we kep him in the rooad all the way up and stopped him at the top; but it wer a very nigh goo for all an us."

Stokenchurch, 1926:

"I went down the roo-ad this morning and called in at the Reeaven."

Brill, 1920:

"Be quick, or else you'll be too laiat for the treean."

"Whosen geeas be they?"

The use of *goo* for "go" is very general, and seems equally prevalent in large towns like High Wycombe, Chesham, and Aylesbury. Five decades of elementary education have passed, with insistence upon the modern conventional sound in the class-room, but as soon as the restraint of school is over the majority of scholars revert to the older form in the playground. I have listened to the shouts during recreation in many schools all over the county, but to hear any scholar say "go" immediately attracts my attention as unusual. In 1923 I even heard *goo* at Wolverton, a place where it might least be expected owing to the influx of population from other parts of England. The following incident is an example from the extreme east of the county:

Chesham, 1923 (Germain Street School):
On a breaking-up afternoon the boys who were to leave that term were being reviewed.

HEADMASTER. "Mr. Cox, is this boy placed?"

MR. COX. "I have a situation in view for him; he must first be seen."

HEADMASTER. "When will you go, my boy?"

BOY. "I shall *goo* to-morrow morning, sir."

HEADMASTER. "How many times have I told you to say *Go*!"

Plenty of other examples of the *oo* sound are available:

Steeple Claydon, 1923:
IRATE MOTHER (to child teasing his little sister). "Let her alooan!"

Radnage:
"I dooant like my mait well done; I like it sooar."

The word for sloes (the fruit of the blackthorn, *Prunus spinosa*) is very interesting. On the Chiltern ridges, in such places as Downley, Ibstone, etc., it takes the form *sloo-as*; to the north-east of the county *slons* is more general, and on the west *slans* is frequently heard. The last form is a double plural from Old English *slah*, *sla*, plural *slan*; this in modern dialects has been regarded as a singular and a redundant "s" has been added.[1]

A very entertaining remark by an old Gawcott woman illustrates a pronunciation of "tea" now unusual:

[1] See Wright's *Dialect Dictionary,* vol. v, p. 532, *sub verb.*

"I shull say as the gal said when she had hur chap to tay fur the fust time: 'Chap ur no chap, sahcer mi tay I ull, fur burn mi chops I unt.'"

O and A.

The unrounding of the Middle English "o" in modern times is well explained and illustrated by Professor Wyld.[1] He sees traces of it at the present time in *"Gad,* a weakened blasphemy, and in *strap,"* whereon razors are sharpened. A good many examples are still to be heard in Bucks, as the following examples will show:

Wheeler End, three speakers at the Chequers on one evening said:

(1) "I should like to see a good *drap* a raian to-night, fur ivverything can do wi it."

(2) "Thaiur used to be two ole cottages at Chisbridge *crass* rooads, but they be pulled down now."

(3) "The *craps* dooant look up to much, and they wunt till we git a good raian."

At the same place one of the mummers was asked to give the words of the play, and answered, "Thaiur's a deuce of a *lat* an it."

Frieth:

"The window fraiams be *ratten.*"

Waddesdon:

(1) "I a jest bin and got mi ood in fur the *marnin.*"

(2) "Look at the ole gal gooin a-figgutin *across* the rooad."

(3) "A fine, *frasty marnin.*"

[1] *History of Modern Colloquial English,* 1925, pp. 240-2.

Drayton Parslow:

(1) A game at whist: "That wer a *saft* trick."

(2) A gardening class: "Please, can I *lap* the trees this afternoon?"

Quainton:

SPEAKER (to workman fixing the posts carrying the electric cables to Waddesdon): "How fur a ye got wi the postes?"

"As fur as Waddesdon *crass* rooads."

West Wycombe, 1926:

(1) "I heeur thaiur were two bad *crappers* in Wycombe."

(2) "Did ye no-atice that ther reek bi the side a the rooad as a *drapped* in?"

Dagnall, 1927:

"It ain't very saisonable weather, and it wunt be till we git a few sharp *frastes*."

From my own experience this unrounding of the "o" is much less used north of Watling Street; this seems a very arbitrary division, but in company where it might be expected at Wolverton, Woughton, Simpson, Woolston, and Newport Pagnell, I only remember hearing it at Ye Olde Swan, Woughton, and the speaker was a man from Steeple Claydon. On the other hand, as far to the north-west as Tingewick and as far south as Wraysbury, I have heard it in every place where I have happened to be.

E and I.

There seems to be something of a similar tendency to change "e" or "o" to "i" in the district north of Watling Street.

Thus in the course of a few days the following pronunciations were given by the scholars of Woughton and Simpson Council School:

Gard*in*, fagg*it*, magg*it*, jack*it*, and Will*in* (Willen). A boy from Stokenchurch or Haddenham would have pronounced them: Gard*un*, fagg*ut*, magg*ut*, jack*ut*, and Will*un*, the "u" having the sound which it bears in the word "put."

An exception to this is found in pronounced dialectal villages, such as Haddenham and Wheeler End, where the word "feet" is pronounced *fitt*.

At Princes Risborough an old man was referring to the path which leads from the road to the Baptist Chapel, and said: "As soon as ivver I put mi *fitt* an this path, I be as good as the rest an em."

Similarly the word "seed" is usually *sid* in the Vale, and the word "seen" becomes *sin*.

The word *ivver* is itself an instance in which "e" becomes short "i" all over the county.

At Wheeler End an old inhabitant told a new-comer that he needed a "cestern." When asked if he meant "cistern," he replied, "We dooant say *cistern* up heeur, we allis say *cestern*."

II.   DROPPED, ELIDED AND REVERSED LETTERS

"W" is very generally dropped before vowels, and we find: *ooman* for "woman," *ood* and *ood'us* for "wood" and "woodhouse," and *ool* for "wool." These may be confined to the more remote villages, but *ood* for "would," and *ull* for "will" are general; occasionally *unt* for "won't" is heard.

The "w" is also elided in such words as *backurds, forrurds, downurd,* and *uppurd*; and from "athwart"

making it *athirt*, with the meaning "across." "Y"
is dropped from "yes," becoming *ees*, and from
"yonder," which resolves itself into *ender*. "D" is
never heard in the word "grindstone," an example is
from:

Radnage, 1925:
    "Cam an, boey, an tarn the grinstooan."

It is often said that Bucks people never sound the
aspirate and seldom sound the dentals *d* and *t*. There
is some foundation for this, for if any labourer started
to pronounce his *h*'s when talking to his fellows, it
would certainly attract notice, and perhaps be con-
sidered a mark of affectation. As to the *d*'s and *t*'s,
one fears there is a decided tendency to drop them.
The stock example usually chosen by those who want
to laugh at us is: "A liul bi of buhher," which is
intended to convey "A little bit of butter." This
sloppy diction may be heard at times anywhere; [1] it
is admittedly a departure from Received Standard
English, but it is not so much a dialectal characteristic
as a lazy habit.

"The habit of omitting initial *h*," says Professor
H. C. Wyld,[2] "is common to all Regional dialects
except those of the North." It is not proposed in the
following pages to record all these dropped letters;
to do so would merely irritate the reader without
serving any useful purpose.

To dispose of the matter, I will mention the remark

---

[1] This tendency is spreading everywhere, even in America.
The substituted sound is not a full " h " perhaps ; it is known
as the " glottal stop."
[2] *A History of Modern Colloquial English*, p. 296.

of a Granborough girl, after travelling from Winslow to Whitchurch by omnibus: "We a oo gi ow an walk up Urdlegro Ill," which, being translated, is: "We had to get out and walk up Hurdlegrove Hill."

To hear *haps* for "hasp" ("Jest haps the duur") and *wops* for "wasp" is usual. A word which will be found in the Glossary at the end is *clapse*, a contrivance for fastening cows in a milking-shed. This is undoubtedly another form of "clasp"; in the plural it is a pure dissyllable: *clapses*.

"Ask" is commonly rendered (and spelt here) as *ax*. The sound can be seen preserved in a letter [1] written on 12 May 1480 by Thomas Granfyld (that is, Grenville) of Stowe, the great-great-grandfather of Sir Richard Grenville: "Thomas Hayward came to me . . . and acsyd myne avyse what was beste to do."

III. PRONOUNS

The first person singular pronoun is often sounded as e; the following are instances:

West Wycombe:

"Are you going to the Flower Show?"
"No, that e baint."

Stokenchurch, 1925:

FIRST GIRL. "You be out."
SECOND GIRL. "No, that e baint."

Aston Abbotts, 1925:

A. "You here agen! Ant ye had yur dinnur?"
B. "No, that e baint; ant ye had yourn?"

[1] *Stonor Letters and Papers*, 1919, vol. ii, p. 104.

A. "No, e be jest gooin to have it, and then e be gooin to see the crickut match."

West Wycombe, 1925:

"How's your bronchitis now?"

"E be much better than what e was. E always gits it at the beginning o' winter, so this year e went under the doctor and got better, but jest as e was well e got a cold and started it agen."

Drayton Parslow, 1926:

TEACHER. "Look, here are two pages unfinished."

BOY. "Please, sir, e didn't notice em."

The use of the objective *her* for the nominative "she" is certainly much diminished and likely to disappear amongst the younger generation. I have a note of a good instance of its use in 1923 when the district nurse of Tingewick was visiting a patient near Water Stratford; the husband of the patient said: "Her doant know how bad her be."

The use of *en* or *un* for "him" is often found.

West Wycombe, 1926:

"There seem to be very few hares about now."

"I only know of one on my ground, and his usual run is down my fields, across your meddur and along tords Starve Hall. If I'd a gun in my hands tother day I should have shot en."

Quainton:

"We were gooing acrass the feeuld when the dog bolted a rabbut and caught un afure he reached the hedge."

Stokenchurch:

"I saw en coming up the rooad."

"Themselves" is very generally rendered by *ther-selves*. The following dialogue, written by a Wad-desdon girl, serves to illustrate faithfully this and other points of dialect:

A. "Wal, ole meeat; an ow's yur gardun a-gittin an?"

B. "All right, me boo-ay, me teeators be a-gooin an fine."

A. "Do yur booays elp ye?"

B. "Ees, th' be good boo-ays, but th've had sich colds leeatly."

A. "Ah, me wife an the two childern have had it su bad th' dooant know what to do wi therselves."

B. "Ull ye come roun th ouse an have a glass a wine?"

A. "Ah, that e ull, ole chap."

B. "Cam an then, me wife is a-meeakin some mince pies; ye can teeak one ur two fur yur missus."

A. "This ere wine's good, meeat; it begins to git up in mi head."

B. "'Tis, the missus is a good un a-meeakin wine."

A. "Well, e shall a to be a-gooin, er mi missus ull be worrited to death. Good-day, meeat."

The possessive pronouns and the relative "whose" are constantly used with a final "n." The following are a few instances noted during the past five years:

Gawcott:
   "There was a little flint as went right through hisn."

Waddesdon:
   "Please, sir, ourn be right and hisn's wrong."

Aylesbury, 1926:
   "That lot's yourn."

Aston Abbotts, 1926:
   A. "What be ye at?"
   B. "Gittin goose-gogs."
   A. "How be yur currants?"
   B. "Our red uns be all right, but black uns be blighty."
   A. "So be ourn."

Wheeler End:
   "Whosen turn?"

Drayton Parslow:
   "Whosen's horse is that as a jest bin put in the meddur?"

Quainton:
   "That's theirn; so leeave it alooan."

IV. VERBS

The forms taken by the preterite tense of verbs are anomalous. Some are purely present tense forms, like *give* for "gave," *see* for "saw," *run* for "ran." Others undergo some vowel change, like *set* for "sat," and *riz* for "rose." *Rid* for "rode," and *writ* for "wrote" would have passed for good English in recent years.

The favourite past tense of "catch" is illustrated by the following remark made at Aston Abbotts: "You *ketched* me once, but I ull warrant you wunt do it agen."

The word "frightened," whether a preterite or a participle, is comonly rendered *frit*.

A preterite formed by a shortened vowel-sound is illustrated by the following remark uttered at West Wycombe: "We were dooin very well till the rain cam an and stopped it."

The abbreviation of "have"

"Have" is commonly abbreviated to "a" throughout the county, both by those who speak a pronounced dialect and by those in whom it is less well marked. Examples are:

Quainton:

STANDARD I BOY. "I a stumped him, I a."

Woughton:

"He wunt a to a that."

This is evidently a long-standing manner of speech, for there is an extremely pious letter from William Roades to Sir Ralph Verney when he was arrested in 1655,[1] which, as Lady Verney says, "was followed by more earthly consolations in the form of a venison pasty." Roades writes: "If it plese god I should a ben happie to have seen you eate part of it at Claydon."

---

[1] *Verney Memoirs*, 1894, vol. iii, p. 234.

V. PLURAL IN -EN

It is generally allowed that the only example of this remaining in Received Standard English is "oxen"; in addition one occasionally hears in Bucks "foxen," "placen," and "horsen." At the still remote hamlet of Bennet End, "peasen" was also in use thirty years ago. "Ashen" can be heard at Grendon Underwood.

One word still very widely used indeed is "housen." In 1923 in Aylesbury a woman said in Cambridge Street: "I wonder how long it ull be afore them housen are finished." Again, in December 1926 a man said: "It freezes as hard as it can. I a bin a-working on them housen as are being put up in Southcourt. It frez my stuff as soon as ivver I put it an the booard."

ADSTOCK

(1923)

A Summer Evening

A. "Good evening."

B. "Good evening." (After a pause.) "Heeur's a cheear, so sit down and taiak it ee-asy; when anybody a bin an his legs all day long he wants a bit uv a rest."

A. "Thenk ee. We have had a good rain and the things ull get on nicely now."

B. "I beeant sure as we shant a some moour, and it wunt do any harm—the gardins can do wi it, and so can the country, for I dooant know what we be a-comin to, as it seems turned upside-down along ivvery rooad. What the eend ull be I dooant know."

A. "'Tis in a bad way unfortunately, but perhaps better times be coming."

B. "And it is about time they did come."

(Entry of third person.)

" Hullo, Tom. I dint see ye this marnin. I come down the laian and leeand [leaned] an the geeat, but coont see ye."

C. "No; I was a-thacking a rick in tuther feeuld."

B. "How be ye a-gettin an wi the house? "

C. "'Tis neeurly done now."

B. "You beeant agooin to live in it yurself, be ye?"

C. "No; its for mi son; and I think it ull do jist right fur him."

B. "It ought to."

A. "Do mushrooms grow about heeur?"

38

B. "Yis; thaiur's a good many plaiaces if ye know wheeur to goo an git em."

A. "A you sin any about yit?"

B. "I se fuur big uns this marnin accoming acrass a meddur; they were them big uns as big as a small plaiat."

A. "They be horse-mushrooms and be good to ett."

C. "I know they be; but we dooant think so much an em as we do a tuthers."

B. "I like em, but ony when they be pink; when they be black they maiak ketchup an em."

C. "I like the blue-stalks best."

B. "And so do I."

A. "What be they?"

C. "They be them as be called blue-stalks. They grow out in the meddurs and the gipsies git no eend an em and sell em in Bedford. They be the best, and most people like em bettur than tuthers. I know I do; and I always taiak ceear to git some when they be about.

"When I was aworkin for my ole master in tuther farm, he said to me one day, 'Tom, if ye ull goo and git some a them blue-stalks, you can a breakfust wi me.' I used to goo out ivvery marnin and git a good baskutful and bring em to the farm. They then started to cleean em and peeul em, and when they had finished that, they took down the fryin-pan and fried a good lot a fat baiacon so as thaiur was plenty a fat in the pan. The wust a mushrooms is they want plenty a fat, and if ye aint got much a that they baint much good. We allus had plenty as we fried plenty a rashurs. Some people fry em in buhhur and some in drippin or margarine or anything else they a got, but gi me rashur fat and plenty an it. That's the way to cook em and you cant bait it."

B. "You cant: I like em fried in rashur fat the best."

C. "Well, I ull tell ye: I went ivvery marnin and got the blue-stalks and then had breakfust, and —— he ett the blue-stalks and I ett the baiacon, and we carried an this pritty gaiam till the frast come and spoilt it."

A. "I should like to taiast some a them blue-stalks. I a nivver heeurd an em befuur. Be they the saiam as the little meddur mushrooms?"

C. "They be about the saiam, I should think."

A. "I doant mind them horse-mushrooms miself. When I was livin at Simpson I went out one evenin to goo to Oofun [Woughton], and as I went along I looked ovur a geeat fur a few minutes and all at once I see under some elm trees in the meddur a lot a white specks an a heeap a rubbish wheeur an ole dungull had stood. I went ovur and had a look, and found twenty or thirty of these big uns—some an em you would hardly git in a fryin-pan. I took one or two of the smallist and freshist home and had em fur breakfust next marnin. They waunt su bad, but they taiasted a bit strong. As I coont git any a the tuthers I used to goo and git a few ivvery day, but in the eend I got a bit tired an em as they lastid right into Octobur; but the wust an it was they waunted sich a lot a fat to cook em in."

B. "They did want some, I ull warrunt."

A. "Howivver, I had a good faid."

ASKETT

(1923)

Churry Pies and Su-ut Pudduns

LITTLE GIRL. "Have you made my cart yet?"

A. "No; I ull maiak it next week, and then you can have it."

(Entry of Second Labourer.)

B. "Aint it clooas! It a bin like this all the arternoon. I had mi jackut off neeurly all day, and I a ony jest put it an to come in heeur. I rickun we shull git a storm afu-ur the night's out, and I shoont be surprised if we git it very soon. My gals a bin a-blackburrying all the arternoon and a come home wi a good lot. They a filled a biggish baskut full and so I suppoase we shull be havin blackburry pies and blackburry pudduns fur the nex few days. But I doant like em! I wunt taiast em. They can have em! I shan't. Lots a people a bin out a-gethering em this arternoon. They come out heeur from Aiuhlsburry and git no eend an em, ispecially tuther side a Meadull. They clambur up the hedges and clah em neeurly all off, so when they be gone thaiur aint many left fur anybody else. Gi me straaburries or churries—they be my favourite fruit; a the two I like straaburries."

A. "I doo-ant; gi me a churry—them big black uns; the real ole Bucks black churry. I think they call em 'Croons.' They can't be bait."

B. "I know em, the big black and the little black. I like the big black fur ettin and the little black fur

41

pies. Thaiur's no churry as can come up to em. Thaiur's nothing I like in this world like a real ole Bucks churry pie as be well pinched. I used t' have em ivvery yeeur when I was young—my mothur allus used to maiak em ivvery summur, but I dooant git em now. Tis like ivverything else, all the ole custums gooin out a deeat. I ull tell ye what it is! Women can't pinch em now-a-deeas, tis too much trouble; and if they could they woont. I a sin em many a time maiad jest like half a moon gooin to the baiakhus an a tin, as many as ten at a time. They looked bootiful—ivvery one pinched up as reglur as clock-wurk. And waunt they good when they were done!"

A. "Ah! that's it; ivvery ole Bucks woman in this part a the country could pinch em once an a time, but they can't do it now."

B. "Then thaiur was the ole churry puddun as we allus had wi broad beeans and biled baiacon. You know it!"

A. "Yis, I know it, but I ant sin one for a good time now. You meean a su-ut puddun wi churries mixed up in it. That's a reeal ole Bucks summur dish, but people dooant have it now."

B. "No, because nine parts out a ten a the women can't maiak a su-ut puddun now-a-deeas as it should be maiad. Thaiur's one thing they cant do—they cant get the right linge when they be mixin up. You want a nice bit a su-ut well chopped up and no gret hunches left in it, then mix it wi the flour, and put in a bit a salt. Then you a got to put the water to it and stir it up well till ye git the right linge, nuther too wet nur too dry, and this is what they cant do. Now it has to be tied up in the cloth as tight as it can be tied, and when it comes out a the pot it rolls out jest like a futball. You can then put yur knife an it and it almost falls a-two. That's when they be good and wuth ettin, and what can be bettur fur anybody when ye a got a nice drap a greeavy from a bit a baif or a rearin baiaked ovur a sahcer of inen and saiage? Tis the finist thing fur anybody, ispecially childern, fur they dooant want much mait ar-ur they a had a good bellyful a that. I tell ye a slice or two aich day puts a colour in the chaiks, and if ivvery gal had em ivvery day, half the chimist shops in the country ood soon be shet up."

A. "They ood."

B. "I dunno what we be a-comin to. Half the things be spoiled in the cookin. You cant find cooks about now like the old women as could maiak up a taiasty dish with a few coppurs, and they had to do it when they got seven or aiaht mouths round the teeable ivvery dinnur-time. That used to maiak the women think as they doant now-a-deeas. All the gals be brought up now to be laiades [ladies]: they maunt durty thaiur hands wi wurk. Wurk's be-neeath em; they be sent to these town schoouls wheeur they larn nothing ony to think therselves better than anybody else, and all the time the poour ole dad is wurkin hard to git enoh to ett. When they a done schooul, what good be they ony to dress up, goo to cinemas, dahnces, whist-drives, and ivverything else an the booard! As fur cookin, they aint gooin to do anything like that, no feear! But when the things be an the teeable, they be as good trenchur-men as anybody else. They cant cook a taiater. Look at the little madam when the poor ole mothur ahsks her to look ar-ur some an the fire a-cookin fur dinnur. Thaiur she stands a-timin em and all the time she's a-twiddlin her heear about, lookin in the glass and full a wool-getherin. She soon furgits what time they ought to be done, and she ant got the sense to try em with a fark. At last she thinks they be done and so she says, 'Mothur; they be done! they be done!—they be done!' and when they be streeand [strained] they be aither as hard as stooans or as pappy as sop.

"And this is jest how all the gals be brought up now. They wunt do housewurk—that's beneeath em. They must git a clark's job or goo in a shop or factury, so as they have thaiur nights off and spend all the money they arn on dress. Thaiur they go a-dashin about the straits, showin off thaiur feathers and tryin to git husbands—and fine wives they maiak when they do git em. They be jest like that dashin gal as got married some time agoo. She was one of these. Soon arter she got married, her husband thought he ood like a baiaked rabbut fur dinnur; so he goos up in town and buys one and taiaks it home fur the next day's dinnur. Befuur he left fur wurk nex marnin he told her to baiak it in the ovun; so laiater an she put it in as she was told. When he come home at dinnur-time he sot down in his cheear and begun to smack his ole chops, as he was very fond a baiaked rabbut and it smelt bootiful. So she went to the ovun, opened it, and—if the ole rabbut dint sit thaiur at fu-urm with his jackut an."

A. "Come, that's too good: you meean to say she nivver took his jackut off?"

44

B. "That's as true as I sit heeur. That's one a these fine laiades as a nivver bin brought up to do house-wurk. Think I ood a one fur a wife! Not me! Gi me a gal as a bin to sarvice and knows how to kaip a house tidy, and look ar-ur the childern, and can use a bit a elbow-graise and allus a got summut taiasty in the cupboard. That's the gal I should have fur a wife if I had my time ovur agen."

A. "You be right. Whoo's a-gooin to win the fight—Beckit or Carpinteer?"

B. "Why, Beckit; he's ony to give him one good sock under the jah and he's done. Howivver, we ull see."

BUCKLAND

(1923)

Old Drover at the Plough

A. "A nice day! The harvist wunt be long if it kaips like this."

DROVER. "It wunt; stiull, a reean ood do good. Tring Show to-morra, and I hope it ull kaip fine fur that. Be ye a-gooin to it?"

A. "No; I haven't thought about it, but I heeur tis a very good show."

DROVER. "Tis; wuth gooin to see, if ony to have a look at the ship-dog triuls. Hunderds goo to see em, as they come from all parts of England. If it's fine thaiur ull be a big crowd. I hope it ull kaip fine, if ony for the holiday-makers at the seaside."

B. "Tis jest the weather for holiday-makin—that is, if ye a got twenty or thirty pounds in yur pockut to spend; but now-a-deeas that doant fall to the laiabourer, so he has to stop at home and do the best he can wiout em."

A. "Yis, times are hard and doant seem to get much better."

B. "Tis the price a things that maiaks it su hard for anybody to git an now-a-deeas. They could be behhur, but tis the profiteerin gooin an as kaips prices up. A man doant git a chance to git anythin, and when ye ant got nauthin in yur pockut nobody thinks anything an ye."

A. "That's the way of the world."

B. "That's quite right: if ye ant got nothin, ivverybody's down an ye."

46

A. "Well, if I had my time ovur agen, I should pack up for Canada."

DROVER. "Or Australia! Do you know anythin about it?"

A. "No; do you?"

DROVER. "I have a brother out thaiur. He's bin thaiur for neeurly fifty yeeurs. When he done his time in the army he went straiaht out and has nivver come back."

A. "What rigiment was he in?"

DROVER. "The ole 43rd, his father's ole rigiment."

A. One of Wellington's old fighting rigiments. Was he in any war?"

DROVER. "The Rooshan and the Indian Mutiny."

A. "Don't you heeur from him?"

DROVER. "I heeurd fuur years agoo, but since then we ant had a wurd from him: we a writ, but can't get any answer. I ixpect he's dead, as he's a good deeul oldur than I be. I should like to know what a become an him, whether he's alive or dead, though I shull nivver see him agen as he ood be too old to travul all the way to England. Howivver, I should jest like to see him once agen as he's my brother."

A. "What is he?"

DROVER. "A gold-miner: when he last writ he said he had struck a bit a luck, but he nivver said in what way. He's got fuur childern, but we doant hear anything from em."

A. "Do you live here?"

DROVER. "I a lived heeur all mi life. I used to live in them housen neeur the church as were pulled down a few yeeurs agoo. It was a sheeam to pull em down, as they were as good as this one is—gret o-ak beeams and as good housen as anybody could wish for."

A. "What a pity!"

DROVER. "It was a sheeam, for they want em now."

A. "Where did the people go?"

DROVER. "Some went down to the new housen, and tuthers left the village; and thaiur were sties for twenty pigs and a donkey-shed as well. That's the way how the poor man's sarved now-a-deeas. You can depend an it they wunt build new pig-sties wi the new cottages, and how can anybody kaip a pig as he used to? Do you live about heeur?"

A. "I come from Wycombe way."

DROVER. "That's the pleeace wheeur they maiak the cheears."

A. "Yes; do you know it?"

DROVER. "I do. I used to go thaiur pritty awfen. The last time I went I took a looad a hurdles for a man naiamed Terry who maiad em by hand. When I see em an the ground ready to be looaded up, I thought to miself, I shull nivver be able to taiak all an one looad. Howivver, he started puttin the staiaks at the bottum a the cart and when he had done that he piled the hurdles an the top and fastened em an. I started and got a mile or so along the rooad when it begun to shift, and I was afreead they ood fall awf. Howivver, I kep an and got to the Halfway House. Do you know it?"

A. "Yes."

DROVER. "So I went in and asked the landlord whether he had a rooap to lend me. He found one, and so we tied em an tighter. I started agen and got through Missindun; then I turned up Nag's Head

Laian and at last got to Peterley. I went athurt Kingshull Common and started gooin down hill. I tell ye, it was one of the biggist jobs I had to keep the looad an, and I felt glad when I got down to the level rooad. The rest a the journey I done all right, but I was glad when I unlooaded at the pleeace wheeur I was sent."

A. "I should have thought Kimbull way was bettur, but I suppose it's a bit longur."

DROVER. "That's the raison why I didn't goo that way. Howivver, I got through, but if ivver I had bin asked to taiak a looad like that agen I ood nivver a done it."

CUBLINGTON

The Feast

A. "Ah! Cubbeltun Feeast aint what it used to be. We did a some good uns yeeurs agoo—we did a some feeastes then. It took us all the waik to ett ivverything up. In th' ole days waiks afuur it come we writ fur subscriptions to the gentry all around, and in ur lehhur we allus invited em to dinnur, an tis wonderful what we got. A coourse we didnt want em to come to dinnur, fur some an us woont a knowed how to goo an at the teeable if they'd a bin thaiur. Any reeate, we allus got plenty a money to git plenty a mait and ivverything else we wanted. We had the big faid the fust day and kep an ivvery day artur till it was all finished. They were some times then! Peepul come from all ovur the wurruld to Cubbeltun feeast afuur the war; the pleeace was filled. In ivvery yard carts and waggonettes wur stored, besides ivverywhere else wheer one could be put. That was afuur the war, but now things be down and thaiur aint th' interest took in it as thaiur was then; but still, it aint a bad un this yeeur."

B. "Cam an! let's git up to th' Unicorn afuur the crowd comes up. We can have a table togither fur a little while; if we dooant, we shant git in fur the peepul when the band stops a-playin." (*To newcomer*) "Hullo! how be ye a-gittin an? What do ye think a the feeast?"

C. "Well, taint a bad un, but we a had behher feeastes in Cubbelton yeeurs agoo."

B. "We did; but taint a bad un this yeeur, an I

50

be glad an it. I dooant like to see the ole feeast goo down. A ye heeurd the band?"

c. "Yis."

b. "I rickun tis a jolly good band. I rickun they play well. We had the Old Un this arurnoon."

c. "What old un?"

b. "Why, the reeal old un uv all—'The Farmer's Boy.' They played it arly in the arurnoon, and some an us as were standin by a-listenin to it did give it bains. We did let hur have it. Talk about music, did ye ivver heeur sich music? Thaiur nivver was sich music. Thaiur's moour music in 'The Farmer's Boy' than in all the music as a ivver bin played put togither. We ull all goo down and ask fur it to be played agen, that we wull! and we ull all sing it togither. We ull ask fur it to be played by special request."

DRAYTON PARSLOW

(1926)

A. "What a night! Tis as dark as pitch. I a jest come up the road and I dint know how to find mi way. I got in the hedge once or twice as I was a-tryin to git out a the way a the pond. This is, I think, about one a the darkest nights as ivver I was in. I could jist see the trees in the hedgerows agenst the sky, and what with the wind a-blowin in the branches and the noise they made, I felt quite creepy as I come up. I shoont like to git fur afeeuld to-night."

B. "You ought to goo down to Sauldin [Salden] an a night like this. That's wheeur you ought to goo, and then you ood see summut."

A. "What?"

B. "Sauldin's a rum ole pleeace, Sauldin is. Tis a rum ole pleeace, I tell ye!"

A. "What do you see?"

B. "Why, a ole fellur with his feeace under his arm —he comes out an a night like this. I tell ye, tis a rum ole pleeace!"

A. "A you sin him?"

B. "Ant I, begad—many a time!"

A. "What does he do?"

B. "Well, I ull tell ye. When you git down tuther side a Sauldin pond an a night like this, and you be a-gooin an the rooad, thaiur's an ole fellur as comes and walks by yur side—thaiur he is a-gooin an by the side an ye, and thaiur's his old feeace under his arm a-lookin at ye all the time, and he keeps an till he gits to a certain pleeace and then he leeavs ye.

52

He walks by yur side all the time and nivver speeaks."

A. "Don't ye crack him an the head wi yur stick?"

B. "No, begad; I allus let him alooan; these things be best let alooan. Besides, he nivver hurts ye. Many a time has he bin by mi side and he nivver does nauthing. When he gits to a pleeace he leeavs ye, and ye dooant see him agen. I awfen see him when I goo a-stoppin the fox-hoales. I tell ye tis dark some nights when I be out and then's the night he comes. Yo dooant see him an moonlight nights. I dooant beleeav in messin about in them things. I beleeav thaiur's summut in his comin like he does. If ye were to follur him, I rickun he ood taiak ye to a pleeace wheeur thaiur's a pot a money or summut like that; but thaiur aint anybody has a got the pluck to goo wi him."

A. "When did ye see him fust?"

B. "One dark night when I was wi ole Tom Kirk. We were an tuther side a the pond when ole Tom says to me, 'Look out, Jim; heeur he is!' And thaiur he was too, a-walkin by the side an us. My heear stood an a eend and lifted mi cap right up. I tell ye I had got the wind up properly. There he kep an by the side an us with his ole feeace under his arm a-lookin at us."

A. "What did ole Tom do?"

B. "Nauthin: all he said was, 'Let him alooan. Taiak no no-atice an him!' Ole Tom had sin him many a time, so he was quite used to him. He lived jest a tuther side a the pond and had walked the rooad all the times a the night, so he dint mind him."

A. "What is he like?"

B. "Well, I ull tell ye. He's dressed summut like an ole-fashioned poleeasman, but not like the cloaths they a now-a-days. Tis a funny dress, but the thing about him is, he's allus had his ole feeace under his arm. Ye know Sauldin's a rum old pleeace. The Wars a the Roses were fought out thaiur. They had some big battles an that ground. Thaiur used to be a big mansion wheeur the sogers used to be kep and thaiur's intrenchments all ovur the pleeace; besides, Sauldin windmill stood till a few years agoo, and this used to grind the corn for the sogers. Nobody knows what happened in them days. Thaiur's not the slightist doubt the ole fellur is one of them ole sogers as fought in the Wars of the Roses and cant rest, but wants to tell somebody summut. I ull tell ye, if anybody had got the pluck to follur him, he ood taiak em to a pleeace wheeur thaiur's a pot a money. But nobody a. Another thing I a heurd my ole fathur say, as when the ole mansion stood the geeats as led up to it allus opened and shut by therselves at twelve o'clock a night, and nobody could opun or shut em arter that time. I ull tell ye theiur used to be some rum gooins-an down at Sauldin."

C. "I shant believe it."

B. "You can beleeav it or not, but that was the ceeas."

D. "Where does the ole fellur come from? Out a the woods?"

B. "I dunno wheeur he comes from; but I ull tell ye when he's out and you goo by the pond you ull find it all of a wurk. That's a funny thing! I a sin it many a time, and when I ant met him and I

54

see the pond all of a wurk, I know he's out somewheeur. He might come out a the intrenchmints,
but I dooant think he comes out a the woods. You
find the 'Chariots' in Sauldin woods."

A. "What be they?"

B. "Why, you ood know if you were a-gooin
through em an a night like this. You heeurd that
fellur as were sittin in that cheeur tuther night speeak
about em. His ole fathur had sin em many a time,
and so have a good many moour. I ull tell ye what
they be! When ye git down in them woods an a
dark night and gooin through the darkist pleeaces,
all at once a chariot, drawn by horses and filled wi
funny ole people, comes dashin up behind and passes
ye like a whirlwind—and they be some funny people
in it too. It clutters up dust and stooans, and I can
tell ye it maiaks yur heear stand bolt upright."

A. "I heeurd my landlord tell the saiam taiul [tale].
He said thaiur was a young chap from Bletchley
started wurkin at one a the Sauldin farms, and the
fust night he walked back hooam through the woods.
It was an awful dark night, and when he got in the
middle, he heeurd sich a row a-comin up behind,
and all at once a funny-sheeapd coach come a-tearin
past him like the wind. It was full a people, and
sich funny-lookin fellurs too, that he was frit out
of his wits. Did he ivver see it agen, says I? 'No
feeur,' says he, 'he nivver went to wurk agen at
that pleeace. Next day he got another job at
Bletchley—he had quite enough that one night.' I
then axed him whether he had sin the old fellur
with his feeace under his arm. 'Well,' says he, 'I
ull tell ye what, I dooant like to speeak about sich

things. I nivver say nothin. Well, I ull tell ye. One night when I was a-wurkin laiat at Swanburn staiation I come acrass Gret Ground. It was terrible dark, and when I got part a the way I see summut a-walkin by the side an me. I tell ye, I was sceeard. Howivver, I kep an, an when I got neeur the stile he left me. I went down to the Three Horseshoes and told what I had sin, and ole —— says, "That's wheeur I see him tuther night, and he left me at the saiam pleeace." I dooant like talkin about these things, but there's summut in em.' "

c. "I don't believe it. I wunt believe such things exist."

B. "You can beleeave em or disbeleeave em, thaiur tis, they be true. It aint one who a sin em—thaiur's scooars who a sin em about heeur. You'v ony to goo down tother side a the pond or in Gret Ground or Penny Hadley, and you ull see all ye want to see. Thaiur's some rum ole pleeaces about Dreeaton. I ull tell ye summut else. One dark night ole —— was comin from Bletchley about twelve o'clock. It was as dark as it could be and he could hardly see his way along the rooad. He had passed Skew Bridge and got nearly to Chaddul [Chadwell], when all at oncce he heeurd a noise like a rigiment a sogers come a-rushin up behind him. They cluttered up the stooans an the rooad and some an em hit him in the back, so he turned round and feeaced em and hilt up a baskut as he had got an his arm to defend hisself. Howivver, they passed, and he went an, sceeard out of his wits. Next mornin he had to goo to Bletchley agen, so he started pritty early. When he got to the pleeace wheeur the horsemen passed him, he looked at the rooad, and thaiur were the stooans in the rooad. What do you think a that! The stooans hit him in the back. Aint thaiur summut in that?"

c. "I shant believe it, Jim. How is it these things always come out at night and never in the day?"

b. "They do. Mr. ——, who lived at the farm wheeur Mr. King now does, one mornin went out along the laian jest round the carner, when he see, as he jest got past the chapul, a funny-lookin man further up, and all at once he disappeared in th' hedge. He waunt like an ordinary man, but it frit him so he nivver went up that laian agen."

a. "Not in broad daylight?"

b. "No! Not in broad daylight. He nivver went up it agen."

a. "That's funny."

b. "That is funny; and I ull tell ye thaiur a bin some funny things happen in Dreeaton. I a sin em wi mi own eyes, so I can't disbeleeave em. That ole fellur with his feeace under his arm I a met scooars uv times. I ull taiak ye down to Sauldin pond one a these dark nights. Will ye goo?"

a. "Yis, I ull. . . . What's the time?"

b. "Why, gittin an!"

a. "I shull have to make a move."

b. "So shull I!"

a. "I hope I don't meet the ole fellur down the rooad!"

b. "He dooant git as fur as this. We ull goo down to Sauldin pond one a these nights and I ull show ye him."

a. "I shall taiak a good stick."

B. "You leeave him alooan; he won't hurt ye. If ye got a-messin him about, thaiur's no tellin what he ood do!"

A. "Well, good night all!"

B. "Good night! Keep your eyes open when you're gooin down. Look well in the hedge!"

C. "Good night, Jim. Shant believe these things you a told us about to-night."

B. "Pleeas yurself. They be all true."

———

A. "Have ye got yur gardins ready yit?"

B. "Partly. The boys a bin at em to-day and dug a good bit up. Thaiur's one thing, they do know how to dig. What they a done, they a done well; tis a credit to em!"

A. "What sids a ye put in?"

B. "We a put in two rows a reddishes, a row a pais, two a carruts, and two a turnups."

A. "Turmuts! What, turmuts?"

B. "Yis."

A. "The County Council a done us a bit a good at last. They a sent us a man as is gooin to git turmuts afuur we set the sids! I can see they be a-gooin to think an us a bit now; and quite time, too!"

B. "How's yourn?"

A. "Ant touched it, and ant a-gooin to yit. Tis too arly to set anything; if e did now e should be no forrader as them as sets a few wiks laiater. I dooant belaive in settin things too arly, for they ony git nipped by the frast; besides, the land's too cold and wet and tis no good a-lettin the sids lay in the ground and not grow. I allus a found that when the sids begin to sprout tis best for em to keep straiaht an. I shant put anythink in till arter the twenty-fust."

B. "Tis time the broad beeans were in! I know some who sets em an the shortist day and they nivver seem to hurt."

A. "I know they do. I nivver grow em!—dooant like em!—nobody in the house do. I nivver have em. I wunt give a penny for a bushul an em if e had got to ett em!"

B. "Well, that's stree-ange; I thought ivvery coun-tryman liked broad beeans."

A. "Well, I dooant, and I wunt grow em at any price."

B. "I a heeurd a some people who ood ett em all day long if they had got the chance. They ull ett em when they be as hard as stooans, and a got eyes as black as night."

A. "I know they ull."

B. "I know somebody as, when they be young, cuts em up, shell and all, like kidney beeans and has em in that way."

A. "Like ole Broad-beean Jack a Gret Horrood as went black in the feeace a-ettin em. I nivver did see anybody ett broad beeans like him; he was allus at it when he could git hold an em. I a sin him many a time wi a baiason full a-tuckin em down as if he ant got a minute to live, and he did shift some when he was about it. He used to have em in that way."

B. "Well, I a nivver tried em like that, but I shall the fust chance I git. I dooant think I shull like em that way so much as I do the beeans therselves.

I like the taiast an em so, and I can ett em ivvery meeul a the day."

A. "And so can a good many moour!"

C. "I like all kinds a beeans. Why, them thaiur haricot beeans as the army had be ony French beeans growed in Egypt and peeuld; they be ixactly the saiam."

A. "A ye started an yur allotment yit?"

C. "No; but I shall as soon as I can while this dry weather lastes; it ull do good to dig it up. I hope to git some an it ready by the eend a the wik [week], and then I shall sow some inens."

A. "How be ye off fur sids! A ye got enoh?"

C. "I a got plenty."

B. "Is it very good soil for inens?"

C. "Yis, the soil suits em well. I had a good crap last yeeur. Some people maiak a mistaiak in puttin coal ashes an the bed. That kills plants. Wood ashes be all right and plenty a sutt, but you daunt want to put that an jist out a the chimley. You want to let it lay by for a time. I put two bushul an ourn last yeeur, and we had as good a bed as ivver we could wish to have."

B. "Gooin to the Point-to-Point at Swanbourne to-morra?"

A. "No, I baint. I shant goo; ant got any money to lose, if e did have e woont goo. I heeur you can ony git in the dinin-tent by tickut this time. I suppoase they a larnt a lesson from that Hogston affeear some yeeurs agoo. I nivver did see sich a sight. I nivver was so ashaiamd a miself as I were that day. I went in the tent to git a bit a lunch, and I see a lot a fellurs I knowed. They waunt

60

smallholdurs nur farmurs, but they got in somehow.
I dooant think they had tickuts, but they were sot
down at the teeables and had a taiast a ivverything
as come an. It dint mattur whether it was baif,
mutton, staiak pie, ham, or anything else, they had
a bit of aich; besides thaiur was ivvery kind a drink
and they sot thaiur and sampuld the lot. When they
could ett and drink no moour, they went out to see
the raiaces. I nivver did see sich a sight and I nivver
was so ashaiamd; they went heeur and they went
thaiur, and at last they had to looad some an em up
in a dungcart. There was ole —— with his head
a-hangin ovur the taiul-booard jist like some ole yoe.
Thaiur wunt be anything a that to-morra, I ull tell
ye that. I heeur admission is by tickut."

D. "I a got one. Thaiur were fuur an us in the
feeuld yisterday mornin when we met the secretary,
so we axed him for one apiece, so he says, 'Got gardins,
I suppoase!' 'No,' we said; 'we are smallholdurs.'
He give aich an us one, so I shall goo and have a look
round."

C. "Is thaiur many gooin from Dreeatun?"

D. "I ant heeurd as many are gooin, but I ixpect
a good many ull goo. If it's fine, it's a good day's
outin."

C. ("Wait a minute, Meeary; I ull pay ye. I a
got my money all mixed up in mi pockut wi broad
beeans, kidney becans, and hay sids.")

A. "Shall ye goo to the lunch?"

D. "I daresay I shall have a little if e can git hold
an it."

A. "Well, tis a standin-up touch this time, and
nobody ull git in wi'out a tickut, and a good job too.

They wunt a that Hogstun touch ovur ageean, so if anybody wants to maiak a beeast a hisself this time, he ull a to do it a-standin up. I nivver was so ashaiamd a miself as I were that time to see people maiak sich hogs a therselves and I soour I ud nivver goo agen."

(*The conversation changes on entry of fifth person.*)

A. "Hullo, Tom; bin hard at it?"

E. "Bin an done a little bit. I kep an as long as e could. I a dug a nice bit up, so I maiad a very good start. Pint, Eli! I ull sit down ovur heeur."

A. "You ull find it a bit warm jist thaiur."

E. "Nivver mind, I shull be all right."

B. "They had a very good company at the concert on Sa-urday night, I heeur. How much was took?"

E. "Why, ovur ten pounds, and thaiur's moour to come. I dooant think the ixpenses ull come to much, so they ull cleeur a nice little bit. We kep that down as much as we could, fur we went next mornin an cleeand up the rooms. We shifted all the deskes and cleeand up ivverywheeur, so nobody cant complaian as we dint leeav the schooul as we found it."

B. "What is the money for?"

E. "Why, for the childern's sports at the Feeast. It a got to goo to buy em prizes."

D. "That ull fall through like ivverything else. Thaiur's nobody to taiak any interest in sports in Dreeatun. I nivver did see sich a pleeace. Cant git nobody to do nothin at all. Ivverybody wants somebody else to do all the wurk. They wunt do anything therselves. I know they ull fall through."

62

E. "I know they wunt."

D. "I know they ull. Who is thaiur, then, as ull do it?"

E. "Be you 'Ole Moore' prophesyin as thaiur wunt be any sports?"

D. "Thaiur wunt be any."

E. "I know thaiur ull. If we a got to rely an you to help, thaiur wunt be any. Last time when you were put an the committee you nivver attended a meetin. You ull see!"

D. "We ull when the time comes."

B. "When is the Feeast?"

E. "On Trinity Sunday—the Church anniversary."

B. "I suppoase you have a good time?"

E. "We do, allus have had; but not sich a good time as they had yeeurs agoo. They had a fine time then. Thaiur were two feeastes then, the Monday feast and the Tuesday feeast. The Monday feeast was the Cock and Hen feeast. They were times then! That was the ony holiday a the year fur the peepul a Dreeaton. They seeavd up thaiur money for wiks afuurhand, and many an em kep it up all the wik. They used to a two bands, one an Monday and tuther an Tuesday. The night afuur the stall-holdurs used to goo and choose ther pitches up the rooad and on the green ready fur the next day. They used to be all the way up, and sold all kinds a things to ett. Ole Meead from Stutely used to bring his swingin booats, and I tell ye, he did do a traiad; as soon as he a got a boo-atful and set it a-gooin, he used to sing, 'Fal-lal-lal, Fal-lal-lal, Fal-lal-lal' about three times and then let it die down, so many were standin by and wanted a swing. Peepul come from ivverywheeur, the pleeace was full, and the public-houses were crammed all day. They used to have ooak boughs tied to the duurpostes and ovur the lintul."

B. "Is that done now?"

E. "No, that a bin done away wi fuurteen or fifteen yeeurs agoo at the Horse and Jockey."

B. "That was a fine ole-fashioned custum, and tis a pity that they dont do it now. What bands did ye have?"

E. "Sometimes the Wing band, sometimes the Stuteley band, and sometimes the Bletchley band—had a different band aich day. We used to meet the Wing or Stuteley band at the Potash and the Bletchley at the bottum. We had got our bannurs, and then we marched through and visited the vicar and the farmurs in turn. Ivverybody was pleeased fur us to visit em, and they give us home-brewed beeur, and then the band plaiad an the green. You should a sin how the old men danced and caiaperd [capered] about—twas the ony holiday they had in the yeeur. They used to dance, and I ull tell ye what they did. They brought these 'monkeys an the sticks' and pushed em up and down as the band plaiad. They did injoy therselves, I tell ye. Thaiur aint sich times now as thaiur were then. They had ther dinner, and the nex day they went and cleeard up what was left. Many an em dint goo to wurk that wik; they kep it up all the time. That was the ony holiday they had in the yeeur, and they maiad the best an it. Now, tis ony one day, an the Monday, as the clubs got pritty low. They spent the club funds for the

feeast and at last they had to hand em ovur to the
Oddfellows. That is why thaiur is ony a Monday
feeast now."

B. "If a be anywheeur in the district, I shall come
to Dreeaton an that day."

A. "Yis, come. I ull gi ye a bit a grub, but you
maunt ixpect any convainience, as we shull be full."

B. "I shull come if I can."

A. "Right you are; I shull have a bit a bread and
chaise in the cupboard for ye."

Interview with Mr. Bates

"I BE ovur eighty yeeurs uv age, so I remembur the
fifties. I waunt very old then, ony a boey, but I
remembur em well. They were hard times and
hungry too; ivverybody was at their wits' eend how
to maiak eends meet—and they had big families in
them days. Thaiur's one thing, they hardly ivver
see any mait, and how could they, when tay was
fuur shillings, sugar tenpence, and bread a shilling a
looaf? Howivver, they brought up the childern
somehow, and they growed into strong men and
women—strongur than what they be now-a-deeas.

"It was a hard mattur to faid em, as thaiur waunt
so much wurk about as thaiur is now, and very little
money as well. Bisides, Dreeaton was a biggur
pleeace then what it is now. In my time I can remembur between thurty and forty housen being
pulled down, and they waunt put up agen. Times
be cheeangd—and fur the better too. Nearly ivverybody wurked in the village; very few, if any, went

to other pleeaces, as they were too fur away. So thaiur was allus plenty a laiabour. I went to wurk as a boey at a shillin a wik at six o'clock in the mornin, and the horsekaiper had ony eight shillins, and he was allus a-milkin the cows when I got thaiur at six o'clock. People were allus out a wurk.

"When threshing time was an, I a sin many a time a lot a strong fellurs awaiatin outside the geeat, hopin to be put an. When the master come out, he used to say, 'I ant got anythink fur ye to-day,' and so went in the barn to look arter things. Howivver, the men dint goo away, but kep a-waiatin about. Sun arter he ood come out and say, 'Now then, Tom So-and-so, off wi yur jackut! Kaip yur eyes opun! Slip in to 't! A shillin a day.'

"Ah! they were hard times! Men wi no money, and nivver shuur uv a job for any length a time.

"I knowed one man who went moast a the way to Ee-aton to git a faggut a ood wheeur the hedge was broke and a lot a ood was dead. He started pritty laiat, so he dint git hooam till artur midnight. As soon as he got indu-urs, his wife started a-maiakin some dough to maiak a ceeak [cake]. They lit the fire and baikd it, and as they ant had much food in the day, they started to ett some an it when it got coldur. I went in th' house the next day and see the ceeak, so I said, 'You a bin busy!' So he said, 'Yis; I went lahst night to Ee-aton and got th' ood and mi wife maiad some dough and baiakd it.' That's how some a the poor folk went an in them days. Tis bettur now, and a good thing too. I remembur my mothur, one feeast-time, buying a pound a baiacon fur all our family; people dooant goo an like that now-a-deeas. Some people say, 'Gi me the good ole times!' I say, 'If they waunt em, let em have em!' I went through em and I dooant waunt to goo through em agen.

"Come a little furdur up the gardin and have a look round."

" The soil looks good."

"Tis; plenty a looam; a good strong soil. It lays feeurly dry too, as the subsoil is gravel; thaiur's plenty a that about heeur. Philip Baiats [Bates], as lives in that pleeace thaiur, dug a good lot out uv his gardin and sent it to Newton. It goos right down as fur as Bletchley. When I buried mi brothur at Fenny, they dug a gret heeap out a the greeav [grave], and that was good land—good corn land; it was a shaiam to a that fur a cemetery."

"Yur trees look well!"

"They do very well; sometimes we git a good crap a plums. That tree next the house is a churry tree, but the churries arnt a good class, as the tree comes frum a pip we set about thurty yeeurs agoo."

FINGEST

(1927)

A (A STOKENCHURCH MAN). "We doant git much rain. It a bin a-threatenin all day and it wunt come. I shull be glad to see it as the time's a-gittin an—the garduns and the craps want it badly."

B (A NATIVE). "Yis, we want it bad! We can do wi a good raian ivvery week in Vingist, as the soil is pritty light, and what doos fall, ispecially at this time a the year, very soon gits away."

C. "What subsoil a ye got down heeur?"

B. "Why, chalk; and it aint very fur down nuther, and so whativver falls very soon runs away through the ground, and that's why we want raian ivvery week."

A. "That's a bit different to what tis up at Stoaken, as moast a the ground up thaiur's clay, and so whativver falls stays an the ground tiull it dries up. You can't dig the garduns up thaiur ivvery day a the week. You a got to be a bit ceeurful, as if the soil's a bit damp you ull nivver break up the clumps a dirt all the summer if you tread an the ground then."

C. "I be a bit surprised as you a got clay up at Stoaken. I should a thought it ood a bin chalk."

A. "Well, anybody ood a thought so, bein as it is an the top a the hiulls, but tis neeurly all clay, but you doant a to dig very fur in some plaiaces afuur you come to chalk."

B. "Well, tis pritty clooas the surfice a the ground in Vingist." (*To Stokenchurch man*) "How fur did ye a to dig afuur ye come to it when ye were diggin the foundation a them housen ye are puttin up?"

A. "Why, ony nine or ten inches."

B. "I thought so; I know that meddur well. Thaiur's very little soil wheeur ye be putting em up, but lower down you ull find a nice depth. I suppoase the raian a washed the soil down to the bottom."

C. "Are you speaking about those two houses at the corner of Turvulle road?"

B. "Yis, jest agenst Vingist House, wheeur one rooad goos to Turvulle and tuther to Skurmut."

C. "I cant make out howivver the people in Vingist House allowed them to be built. I should a thought the land was theirn. It ull spoil the look a the villidge."

B. "They coont odds it. The people as bought the meddur be putting up the housen."

C. "Still, there's one good thing about em—they are having tiles on the roof instead of sleeats. I a jest had a look at em on my way heeur from Turvulle. Wheeur does the Court lay?"

B. "Why, right a the back a Turvulle. You turn to the left jest afure you git into the villidge and the rooad taiaks ye up by the Court to South End."

C. "The Court's haunted, isn't it?"

B. "They say so, but I a nivver sin anything miself. I a heeurd a good many say they a."

C. "So plenty a sin it, a th'?"

B. "Th' say th' ave. I dooant belaive in sech things. If I was a bit narvous like some, I might a toald a differunt taiul. I a bin out all hours a the night, all ovur the pleeace—along the rooads, through the woods, and acrass the feeulds; but as for miself I a nivver sin nothing a the kind."

c. "What kind of a ghost is it?"

b. "Why, tis the ghoast of ole Laiady Brandon. She lived up in Turvulle Court once an a time—how long ago I dooant know. They say she generally rides a white harse and most alwiz comes out a nights; but sometimes she gits about in the daytime. You can alwiz tell hur by the rustlin of her silk dress."

c. "So plenty a sin hur, a th'?"

b. "I dooant belaive in these things. I a nivver sin hur, but when ye heeur so many say th' ave, it maiaks ye taiak a bit a noatice a what th' say. Thaiur was ole Daiavid Sewell, who was one day neeurly frit out of his wits in broad daylight. One arternoon he went up in Church ood to git a faggut a ood. It waunt very long afuur he got a nice bundle, and so he tied it up. He was jest havin a look round when he heeurd a rustlin noise, and turnin round to lift the faggut up an his shelder, he see ole Mother Brandon sittin an it, and she woont let him ketch holt an it nuther."

c. "Well, what did he do?"

b. "Why, got out a th' ood as quick as he could. He nivver furgot it. I heeurd him tell the taiul many a time."

c. "Then he come away wi'out the faggut. Didn't he goo back agen for it?"

b. "He nivver said anything about that. Th' say thaiur used to be another one as used to walk about round that barn halfway from heeur up to Luxter's Hill. He come out soon artur it was dark, and sometimes he walked up and down the rooad and sometimes he was dodgin round about the barn; but the report goos as he was a man as stole the common lands away from the poour, and now cant rest for what he done. I a nivver sin him, and I a bin pahst the barn many a dark night."

D (A TURVILLE MAN). "Well, I a ony had one experience in these things. I a heeurd a good many speeak about the ghoast at Turvulle Court and I lived up thaiur fur ovur a yeeur. I a bin up and down the rooad all times a the night and all round the house and in the trees, so if she had bin about I should a sin hur. Well, one dark night my missus and me were comin down the rooad, and all at once we see summut pass us and heeurd the rustlin of a silk dress. My missus neeurly fainted, and as I hilt her up, I turned round to see what it was, but I coont see nothing. It maiad me feeul a bit funny jest for the minute, but it propurly upset the missus and she nivver furgot it."

A. "That's summut like I had happun to me at Radnidge some time agoo. One night arter it had got a bit dark, I was awalkin down the rooad with my wife not fur frum the chapul, when somebody pahst us. We boath said 'Good night,' but boath an us felt streeange; so we loked round to see who it was, but coont see nothing at all. I belaive thaiur's moour in these things than what we think thaiur is."

B. "Well, I a nivver sin nothing miself. I rickun if ye went to the bottum of em all they could be ixplained. When I see a ghoast I ull belaive in em, but I wunt until I do. Taiak that ghoast as used to come in the churchyard jest opposit yeeurs agoo. Ivver so many see it and hahlf the village were frit out a ther

wits when they had to pahss that way an a dark night.
Well, thaiur was ole ———, and he meant to git to the
bottum an it. So one dark night about eleven
o'clock, wiout tellin anybody, he left his house and
startid to walk acrass the churchyard by the path.
It was a hunkid dark night and the trais [trees]
maiad it darkur inside, but he went gently an. He
could see jest a little way in frunt and the outlines
a the church and tops a the trais agenst the sky.
He thought to hisself if thaiur is a ghoast, tis jest the
very night fur him to be about, as thaiur waunt a
sound to be heeurd anywheeur. So he went and
stood neeur the poarch, and nothing whativver turned
up. To maiak a good job an it, he thought he ood
goo all round the church, so he walked round thaiur.
All at once summut muv, and then he could see the
ole ghoast standin stock stiull jest in frunt an him.
He nivver ixpected to see that and he begun to feel
a bit narvous, so he thought it ood be the best thing
to git out a the way as quick as he could. They
stood thaiur a-lookin at one another fur some time.
He thought if he turned round the old ghoast ood
jump an his back, so he started walkin backurds. As
soon as he muv, the ghoast muv too, and follured
him up, and kep an tiull he got to the frunt a the
church.

"Well, when he raiched the futpath, he waunt very
long afuur he was out a the churchyard. He goos
and calls his naiahbours up and tells em what he had
sin; so they dressed and got canduls and lamps and
sticks as well, and then they all went togither along
the path to the church. When they had got a little
way they could jest see the ole ghoast a-standin in

the dark.   As they got up to him they found it was
a donkey with a whitish-grey cooat as had bin a
graiazin in the meddur near the churchyard and had
got in somehow ur nuther.   I can tell ye if all these
things could be sifted to the bottum, thaiur ud be
summut a this kind as ood crap up and ixplain ivverything.   I shant belaive these things until I a sin em
miself."

GAWCOTT

(1925)

A Storm

WOODMAN. "We be gooin to have it. Hearkee, how it rumbles. It lays ovur Claiadun [Claydon], and when it comes frum that direction we alwiz git it at Gawcutt."

B. "Well, it ull do good; tis jest what we want, for we ant had but li-ul reean laiatly and ivverything wants it."

C. "Yis, ivverybody wants it; but it's too laiat for the pais and the beeans, as they be almost all ovur."

B. "That's a big flash; tis forked lightnin; somebody a got it! It maiaks them people as live in thecked housen a bit narvous, for they nivver know what might happun in sich a starm as this; tis almost as bad as tuther Friday. I was at Bletchley when I see it comin ovur. We had it bad enough thaiur, but I could see it was wuss ovur Buckinghum, as all about that part it looked as black as night. When I got back I found it had been pritty bad."

WOODMAN. "I was out in Gawcutt ood when that was an, and it was about as bad a storm as ivver I was in. I went in th' hut out a the reean, and while I was thaiur, I see the lightnin teear the bark awf uv a trai and throw it a dozen yards away. It come down in torrunts, but not so bad, as I heeurd em say, at Bister, wheeur it come down in buckutfuls and flooded the stret in some pleeaces some two or three foot daip. I always like to git under sheltur

74

when a starm is an, fur you be nivver saiaf under trais, ispecially ooak and ellum—and Gawcutt ood is mostly ooak."

B. "Tis a bit risky to git under ooak and elm, but I a heeurd em say that lightnin nivver strikes a baich tree, and from what I a sin in the Chilturns, it seems pritty true, as I a nivver sin one struck and I a nivver knowed anybody as have."

C. "Tis gitting nearur. How it's a-comin down! The taiators ull come an now. This is what we wanted a few waiks agoo."

B. "How many oods are thaiur about heeur?"

WOODMAN. "A good many. Thaiur's Gawcutt ood, Tingick ood, Charndon ood, and Grindon ood."

B. "Is that Charndon wood as lies ovur agenst Finemore?"

WOODMAN. "Yis."

B. "All oak, I suppose."

WOODMAN. "Neeurly all an it; thaiur are a few other kinds, but very few. They cut neeurly all an it down in war-time—all the fine old trais, and now thaiur's ony young trais left. It belongs to the Bister Hunt, but ivvery membur dooant shoot in it."

B. "Have ye got many burds down thaiur?"

WOODMAN. "Plenty a varmin—badgers, wissuls, sto-ats, jays, gah-crows, and a few magpies."

D. "Any hawks?"

WOODMAN. "We git a few at times. But the most mischeevous of all be the jays. I a got quite a string an em strung up outside mi hut, but them thaiur grey squirruls be almost as bad as the jays. They a killed neeurly all the little red uns, and the ood was full

75

an em a few yeeurs bahk. I ant sin one fur a long time. These grey uns be jest like gret rats. They ull ett eggs and rabbuts too. You cant kaip anything from em. I had one in a trap tuther week, and he gnahed his leg right awf and got away; afuur that I see a fox goo up to one in a trap and gnah his head right awf. We a got a few heears and some pheasants, but plenty a rabbuts."

B. "Any snakes about?"

WOODMAN. "Plenty a sneeaks. You see thaiur's plenty a undergrowth and not many peepul about, so they dooant git much disturbed; but when we a bin a-fellin I a sin our fellurs cut em in two wi a axe. A few days agoo I see one two foot long crawl in a stack a fagguts, but I waunt quick enough to git him. I ull tell ye what I see once. Some time agoo, we went a-furrutin, another chap and me. We put the furrut down a hooal an soon artur a rabbut bolted, and jest as it got to the mouth a the hooal, a goodsized sneeak come out too and wrigguld in the grass. I killed the sneeak and mi maiat collured the rabbut, but I thought that was a funny thing for a rabbut and a sneeak to be in the saiam hooal. Nobody ood belaive it, but it's quite true."

B. "What kind be they?"

WOODMAN. "Why, the long uns be grass sneeaks; but we find a few addurs at times; these aint so long as tuthers. Them thaiur little sqaiking owls be a nuisance as well. They ought nivver to a bin let out in the country. They be ivverywheeur."

B. "Do they eat eggs?"

WOODMAN. "Yis; and anything else they can git hold an. The wust a them be they be out night and

76

day, always an the look-out fur summut to kill. I
a shot a good many. I cotch a white un in one mi
traps (twaunt one a them little uns) a few weeks
agoo, and was jest a-gooin to kill it wi a stick when
Mr. Smith, who was wi me, said, "Dooant kill it!"
so I let it goo. If he ant a bin wi me it would a
bin tied up wi tuther varmin outside th' hut."

B. "I suppoase ye a got plenty a foxes?"

WOODMAN. "We preserve em fur the huntin. It
costs thousands a pounds to kaip it up ivvery yeeur.
Look at the hunters what are kep, and the dogs at
Stratton Audley. Besides, the Hunt gis us a suppur
ivvery yeeur. We a ro-ast baif, mutton, staiak pies,
taiators, greens, batter puddun, and ivverything else,
besides plenty a beeur and whisky. That alooan must
cost pounds, for ivverybody connectid with the Hunt
goos. Thaiur's the ai-agent, kaipers, oodmen, and
ivverybody else all thaiur."

B. "The storm seems to a missed us; it lies more
ovur Lemborough, and I ull warrunt they a got it
theeur and Buckinghum as well."

WOODMAN. "We shant git much more an it; it
dooant reean so hard and the moon is a-comin out.
I shull sun a to goo."

B. "Did ye goo to Preston feeast yisterday?"

WOODMAN. "Yis. The pleeace was crowded;
ivverybody from Gawcutt seemed to goo, besides
many people from Tingick, Ratley, Buckinghum,
Chitood, and Hillesdun, as well as frum other
pleeaces."

B. "Were there any stalls in the village?"

WOODMAN. "Theeur's nauthin a that now-a-deeas;
only the Marsh Gibbon band a-playin an the green.

The starm's neeurly ovur, and I shull a to be a-gooin."
B. "Well, we have had a lovely reean."
WOODMAN. "We have. Good night!"

A Sunday Evening's Walk

A. "I dint see ye when I started. I thought ye had gone, an so I come gently along the rooad, thinkin I might meet ye somewheeur. I kep mi eyes ovur th' allotmints, but coont ketch sight an ye, su when I got to th' ood I set fur a time an them logs hopin as ye ood come down the Rackway. Howivver, as ye dint seem to turn up I come gently an back and jest as I got a few yards down the rooad, I ketched sight an ye as ye come out."

B. "We a jest bin fur ur usual walk through th' ood and had a look round. Well, we a had some fine weather leeatly about heeur. What sort a ye had wheeur you a bin."

A. "Well, we had a nice reean last wik, and they say it a done a lot a good."

B. "Did ye git the starm eesterday ar-urnoon?"

A. "No, it passed us; we ony got a few draps. It seemed to lay ovur heeur."

B. "Well, we dint git a drap; it seemed to goo ovur Oovin and Granborough, and I heeur they had it bad theeur. It nivver rout Gawcutt at all. We could do wi a little drap jest now, fur it ood suit the root craps and it coont hurt much now, as the harvist is neeurly all up. I rickun we a had one a the best eeurs we a had fur a long while. It dooant mattur what weathur we git, people alwiz grumble; but this eeur if anybody grumbles, he ought to be ashaiamed a hisself. Theeur was the spring when we had a lot a reeany weather and some laiat frastes, but they dint do much damage. Some a the blossom were cut, but theeur's a good sprinklin a fruit in many pleeaces. The reean, we know, kep an till the beginnin a hay-time, and a good many carried befuur twas fit; but all July was fine—theeur was hardly a shower, and it was the finist hay-maiaking time we a had fur many a eeur. Ivverybody, wi the ixception a the few who started too arly, got ther hay up in the best condition. They coont help it, fur hardly a drap a reean fell. Then in August we a had jest a few showers so as to git the roots an, and all the rest a bin fine. It coont a bin behhur.

"The Hunt started cubbin last wik. They druv th' ood and killed one; they also druv Tingick ood and killed a couple. Theeur's plenty a foxes in Gawcutt ood, fur when the hounds went in theeur seemed to be foxes runnin all ovur the pleeace, but th' undergrowth is too thick at present fur the hounds to do well; when it dies down it ull be a different taiul wi th' ole foxes. Theeur's moour in th' ood than I thought ther were; I deearsay they a come frum other pleeaces. Fur the past two saisons they a nivver druv Gawcutt ood wiout findin. Us stoppers git a point fur ivvery find an at th' eend a th' eeur us git prizes frum the Hunt. Theeur's one thing, if they do find a fox in it, and it goos t' urth in th' ood, that dooant rickun fur a point. The young uns be a bit big now, and so they ull a to kill a few awf: they ood a had behhur luck last wik had theeur a bin all ole hounds; but they had got a lot a young uns a treeaning fur this comin saison. We dooant presarve in Gawcutt ood, but kaip it all fur the foxes; but we git a few heads a gaiam about."

c. "See that rabbut in the ridin! Theeur he is! Cant ye see him? Theeur he goos! I can see him! Cant you?"

a. "No, that e cant! Wheeur is he?"

c. "Lookee! theeur he is! Cant ye see him now?"

a. "No, e cant."

c. "He's jest gone to the side. He's come out agen. Cant ye see him now?"

a. "Ah! I can. I can see him through the bars a the geeat."

c. "Theeur he goos; he's gone back agen."

(The party then look over some allotments.)

a. "Things look pritty well down heeur. They theeur taiaturs look strong."

b. "They do; they be a fresh sort brought out last eeur. My son had a few awf his master and planted em and kep the sid, and tha's wha's come frum em. They do look well; they a got plenty a room to grow, fur I set em wide apart. Tuthers at tuther eend be Arran Chief. The bottum leeavs uv all an em be feeading a li-ul, but tha's ony to be ixpected at this time a th' eeur. All the taiaturs up bi the side a th' ood a done well. That was a nice crap a beeans as you see stacked up—as good a crap as anybody ood ivver wish to have. The reean come jest in time to saiav ivverything, but twas too laiat fur the Charity. Th' allotmints up theeur rest an gravul, and it wants a reean ivvery wik to git things an the goo. Th' arly taiaturs went awf in that hot

80

weather, but I knowed them down heeur stood a behhur chance, as the ground is heavy and holds the moisture longur. I dooant think as anybody a got any raison to compleean an the whool."

A. "I wonder what they be gooin to do wi them ooats."

C. "I suppoase we shull cut em and give em as faid to the cattle."

B. "Did ye see that account in the peeaper about that mohur accident as happund neeur Daventry? I know the pleeace very well—tis jest outside the town. Theeur was a mohur a-gooin along at a good peeace and met a lorry. It tried to pass the lorry, but jest hot [hit] it as it was passin. At the saiam time a big charabanc tried to git in frunt a the lorry and met the mohur-car. The car hot the charabanc and was turned compleeatly ovur. The petrul tank must a bin smashed, fur the car burst into fleeams wi the two men underneeath. The peeaper says the fleeams riz thurty to forty fitt high. It set fire to the back a the charabanc, but the passengurs all got out saiafly; but the two poour fellurs underneeath the car were burned to death. The fleeams were so fierce that nobody could git neeur, but ar-ur a while they got one poour fellur out dead; the tuther was burned to a cindur, and when it was burnt out they reeakd up the remaians and took em to the wurkhus. That was an awful sight, and nobody knowed who they were, but luckily the numbur a the car was not burnt, so the poleeas found out ther naiams. They turned out to be two travullurs frum Essix, a travullin round the country fur ordurs. I ull warrunt theeur was a lot a money burnt wi em.

The rooads beeant saiaf anywheeur now. Wheeur-
ivver ye goo, ye alwiz see somebody a-reeacing along
as fast as his mohur ull carry him. I ood ruthur
walk, as ye dooant know wha's a-gooin to happun
when ye ride in a mohur."

A. "Yu-ur dog grows. He's a-gittin a fine li-ul
fellur. He's as sharp as a needul. Wha's he up to
in th' edge?"

B. "I deearsay he smells a rabbut."

A. "How long ull ye kaip him?"

B. "He ull be gooin back to Stratton bi Christmas,
fur he ull then be big enoh to drah the foxes when
they run t' urth. The Hunt alwiz kaips tarriers like
these to do the drahin. He's jest the size fur that
job, and we look ar-ur him well at hoom. We dooant
faid him too much, but what we give him suits him.
He has alwiz got a drap a cold water bi his side, and
sometimes I give him a drap a milk and a nice cleean
booan; so he thrives pritty well. Theeur's anothur
frum the saiam littur at Pressun, but he eeant sich a
sharp un as ourn is; he dooant git an su well. [*To
dog*] Cam an heeur! I shull a to taiak him hoom,
else he ull git run ovur."

At the Royal Oak

A. "A ye ivver sin a thrai-ul, mastur?"

B. "Some yeeurs agoo I did, but I ant sin one fur
a long time now."

A. "Well, mastur, I a got one in mi barn. Young
Will a bin a-playin about wi it, but he coont git an
at all. He tried, but had to give it up—he waunt

man enough. When ye see Charlutte, ax hur, and she ull show it ye."

B. "I should a liked to see em threshin wi one as they did yeeurs agoo; but, them days be ovur and tha's a thing a the past."

A. "Teeant quite dead it, fur ole Jole Blinkur [Blencowe] a bin a threshin to-day wi one in mi master's barn. He a bin a-dooin the whait as he got awf his allotmint. Teeant ivverybody as could use a thrai-ul, but when ye got a good man an the job, he ood fet ivvery bit a carn out a th' eeurs. Theeur's art in swingin one and it teeaks some time afuur ye git into 't; if ye ant got the knack ye be likely to fet yurself a cut a the head—and a pritty hard un, too. Anybody could larn how to use one ar-ur seeing it done a few times, but it teeaks some time to do it jest as it should be done. At any reeat, tis eeasy to larn hard wurk bi puttin yur mind to 't; practice meeaks perfict, and ye must a that in thrailin, fur it ood nivver do when two men are threshin, a-feeacin aich other, fur one to be allus hittin tuther a the head. That ood nivver do. A good thrailer ull thresh all the kurnuls out quite as cleean as a threshin machine; but a cu-urse it teeaks him longur. I think ole Joe got a bit a tough whait as he were doin to-day, and when ye a got that theeur's shu-ur to be a few grai-an left in the eeurs."

B. "How many sheeavs at a time do ye thresh?"

A. "Why, when ye be a-thrailin bi yurself ye a perhaps three ur fu-ur down layin bi the side uv aich other an the flu-ur. Ye then hot [hit] the swinjul streeat acrass the bunches a eeurs, but the sheeavs must be hot flat wi the swinjul to git the best results. When two men wurk togither two rows uv perhaps half a dozen sheeavs ur moour are pleeaced an the midstid, the eeurs feeacin aich other, and the butts an the outside. Then the thrailurs feeace aich othur and they hot one up, one down, and tis wonderful how they do it—they do it jest like a machine. To git to the middul a the row they ull teeak a step forrud and then backurds and theeur they kaip an all day long. Ivvery now and then one an em ull put the thrail under some an it and tass it ovur fur tuther to hit.

"Yeeurs ago theeur used to be threshin all through the winter in Gawcutt. Theeur was a big barn standin at the back a Thomasson's house and tha's wheeur the lease carn was brought. Whait was threshed fur sixpence a bushul and beeans fur fuur-pence, and the strah had to be tied up as well. Oo-ats and barley cost the saiam as whait. Theeur used to be some good old times then, fur the women as brought the carn were suppoased to do the winnurin. They allis brought some hoom-maiad wine wi em. Some an it wuz rhubub, some wuz slan, some wuz eldern-berry, and some parsnip. And when the thrailurs had done three ur fu-ur peepul's carn, they waunt fit fur much else fur the rest a the day.

"Theeur was a man frum Wulvertun some eeurs agoo come and see me and Ted Richardson at it in ur barn. He sot down an a sack and watched us. Ar-ur a while he said, 'I should like to have a goo; I belaive I could do it.' Well, we let him try, and it waunt long afuur he got the drap an it. So he said, 'I shull meeak me one when I git back hoom.' He was su pleeased wi hisself that he give us a bob

aich and that was the time when beeur were thrup-
pence a pint. Well, we come down in the village
and spent that, fur the public houses were opun all
day. I dint goo back all the ar-urnoon, but leeater
an I had to goo and see to mi horses."

B. "What do ye maiak em an?"

A. "The swinjul is usually maiad a blackthurn ur
whitethurn. That ull do as well as any ood. A
cu-urse ye want th' ood streeaht and tough and hard,
fur if ye git a safter kind it ull split at the eend.
Th' handstaff is usually ash; it dooant mattur su
much wi that, as that dooant a the wurk the swinjul
has. Thaiur's still a few about in the village, but they
be reearly used now, as theeur's no necessity fur em.
The threshin machine a done fur all that, bisides,
nobody goos a leasin—and they woont if they could.
Neeurly ivvery bit a land's laid down to grass. I
suppooase the farmurs think that pays best and theeur
eeant the trouble a ploughin and sowin and raipin;
bisides, theeur's the weather they a got to put up wi;
but the time ull come when some an it ull a to goo
back to the plough, fur turning all the arable land
down to pasture ull soon be the ruin a the country.

"I dunno what they be a-thinkin about. I can't
maiak out what they be up to. If ye goo along the
Tingick rooad, you ull see all the ploughins broke up
and turned into grass. Heeur's a feeuld jest at the
back a the village as good a ploughin as ivver was;
yit it was turned down. And goo along the Bucken-
hum rooad tis jest the saiam. Theeur ain't half a
dozen men employed an all the farms, and yee-urs
agoo theeur used to be five ur six men an aich an em.
Why, theeur's a feeuld down at Lemborough as was

85

broke up in the war and they a kep it so ivver since.
You should see the craps they git awf an it—five
quarter to the aiacre. And tha's what gits ovur me
—fifty bob a quartur fur the whait and foour pound
a ton fur the strah; and yit it dooant pay."

A. "Us a bin a-thetchin a rick down at the bottum
a Bent Hill, and e nivver had sich a job. Us ant got
a dry thread an us, fur us were in the burrah all the
time wi the sun a-pelting down an us. Twas about
the hottist job as ivver e did have. Us had to goo
and cut some willur pegs fur the thetchin. I
sharpund mi bill afuur e went, and mi maiat had
done hisn, but he had ground booath sides, su he
coont git an su well as I did. I nivver grind ony
one side, and tha's the propur way to do 't, fur
when e struck a bough it flew awf fur yards. It
dooant do to grind booath sides, as it wunt cut like
one as a ony bin ground an one side. Well, us got
ur pegs and went streeaht an with the thetchin, and
then they let th' ole cows into the feeuld. As soon
as they see us they ceeam runnin up to us. They
run about the rick, poked ther horns into 't and
maiad no eend a caiapers—they were up to all kinds
a mischief."

B. "Did they eat any?"

A. "No, they play about and do all mannur a
mischief; they allus do to a new rick. Twas a fine
rick and got up in good condition—it nivver had a
drap a reean an it.

"When us had done this, us were called to see the
hay stacked in them Dutch barns along the Buckinghum rooad as were put up last eeur. I nivver did
see sich a job. They maiad a big mistaiak theeur.

They carried the hay long afuur it were dry; then when they thought another feeuld were fit, they carried that and put it an the top a tuther, so as nair a bit an it had any chance to git round, an this is what ull happun in many pleeaces. They cant leeav it till it's dry; they must git it up and not taiak the chance of the fine weathur comin. Theeur ull be plenty as ull be sorry fur scrobblin it up and not waiatin a li-ul longur. Them as a waiated ull be well paiad this eeur.

"Well, when us got theeur I nivver did see sich a sight. The bays were full and they stood up twenty foot frum the ground. I nivver did see anythink like it. A ye bin in a brewery when they a bin a-brewin and the pleeace is full a steeam? Tha's jest like it was theeur. The speeace between the top a the hay and the roof was full a steeam, and it was as hot as any furnace. I could see what was up and what ought to be done—and quick too. So the master says, 'What do ye think an it?' 'Why,' I says, 'you'd behhur git some an it out as it ull soon fi-ur.' He said, 'You'd behher do it then'; so us started and got about twenty ton out a the top. Us put a lot an the side a one bay and some moour out a the next bay on the tuther side and cut holes in aich a the bays, and so I think tis saiavd. But twas a warm job, I tell ye. Us were as black as sutt and waunt sorry to git hoom and cheeange."

A. "Is your hay cut? I be at liberty now, so I can gi ye a hand. I see they a carried that feeuld nex to yourn. Git an wi it as soon as ye can while the weathur lastes, fur we might soon git a cheeange. That theeur rick jest opposit had to be opund, and they seeavd it jest in time, fur it would soon a fi-urd, and theeur's a good many as ull fi-ur this eeur—them as were carried in the reeany weather jest afuur the warm weathur come.   Now-a-deeas they wunt leeav the hay to be maiad.   Cut it down and leeav it alooan fur the fust day, turn it ovur the second, and carry it the thurd—tha's how hay-maiakin is done now. I dooant ceear what anybody says, you cant beeat the ole-fashioned way wi the reeak and fark.   Teeant hay as they knowed it eeurs agoo.   Then it were hay!   You should a sin the women then at work in the meddurs a-maiakin it—turnin it, tassin it, and reeakin it into rows, fur the sun and wind to git right through it.   Ye nivver see anythink a that now. They say laiabour is too deeur, and they think the hay is jest as good fur the cattul."

B. "Did ye ivver heeur of a winrow?"

A. "No, that e nivver did.   E nivver heeurd that in hay-maiakin.   E nivver heeurd sich a wurd."

B. "Well, tis when the hay is pulled togither in rows fur the wind to git through."

A. "Ah! tha's a hatchel; I should say they be the saiam thing.   When us reeak the hay into long rows jest afuur tis put into cocks, us allus call em hatchels; but e a nivver heeurd em called winrows, and e a nivver knowed anybody as did."

Casual Talk at the New Inn

A. "Theeur's one thing, they dooant wurk now-a-deeas like they used to wurk when I was a boey. They could nivver do what we had to do fifty eeur agoo—they beeant strong enoh.   Heeur's George

a-sittin heeur and bin an a farm all his life, and I ull
warrunt he a nivver done a bit a faggin, and another
thing he coont do it if he were put to 't. Fifty eeur
agoo theeur wur differunt times to what they be
now. Mi fathur ony arned nine shillin a wik and
theeur were seven in family, and we had to do an
that; and we did somehow. Livin were hard then
and many a time we had to goo ur-out. Mait was
out a the question; sometimes we had a bit a baiacon
a Sunday, and then we thought urselves lucky. I
went to wurk at eightpence a wik when I were nine,
and were ony too glad to goo to help to git a li-ul
food.

"Leeater an e got riz to two shillin a wik, and that
was when e was fuurteen yeeur a age, then e begun
to think e ought to a jest a li-ul fur miself. Jest at
that time mi shoes hardly hung an mi fitt. The tops
were all broke and the heeuls all wu-urn away so
that boath fitt were beear to the weathur. I were
alwiz wotcherd. The toes were turned up and the
snow lodged an the tops, so the watur went in and
come out jest as it liked. Howivver, I mentioned
to mi mothur that I thought e ought to have a li-ul
a wik to spend. So she said, 'How can I gi it ye out
a two shillins? Yu-ur waiages dooant kaip ye as it
is, so how can I gi ye any? Howivver, I ull see that
ye have a peear a new boots.' Well, soon ar-ur she
bought me a peear and I wore em. It waunt long
afuur e found e were less comfurtable in the new
uns than e were in th' old. They were as chaip a
peear as she could buy, so it waunt long afuur they
let water and e were as wotcherd as e were afuur.
They pinched me and I suffered awful frum chill-

bleeans and that was what e nivver did wi mi old uns.
I dinno what to do, fur whenivver e put em an e
dint know how to walk—mi fitt were crippuld.
Tha's how the youngsturs got an in them theeur days.
Times be differunt now and a good job too.

"Ah! I remembur mi fathur agreein to cut a seven-
ai-acre feeuld a whait, and then we had to fag it.
I had nivver done any a that afuur, but e slipped
into 't the fust day, awurking bi his side. We kep
an up to baiver-time and then restid fur a li-ul while,
but when we riz to start agen, e coont move—I
were su stiff and tired as I dinno what to do. So I
said, 'Father, I can't do any moour, e be su stiff.'
'Oh! can't ye?' he says. 'I ull see to that.' So he
went and cut a goodish stick out a the edge and says,
'Now come along! fur if ye dooant, ye ull git this.'
I got up as best e could, but dinno how to stand.
Howivver, he took his handkercher as he used to
weear round his neck and tied it tightly round mi
loins, and e found e could git an. Well, I went an
as best e could and soon wore awf the stiffniss; so
e went an all day. Tha's how the kids want sarvin
now-a-deeas! They want a good stick round em,
and if they had it pritty awfen they ood be behher
men and women. They a too much a ther o-an way,
and ye deearnt look at em now. Ye a ony got to
spaik and ye very soon git a back answer. That
woont a done yeeurs agoo, but they do jest what they
like now.

"Why, theeur eeant a young fellur in the village
as could goo and do the wurk the young fellurs done
eeurs agoo. Well, we had to do it to live, and we
done it too. Leeater an when I got an tords the

90

twenties, I could fag as well as anybody, and then the shoe was an tuther foot, fur when e was a-wurkin alongside mi dad e maiad him goo sich a peeace as he coont kaip up wi me. Then he used to say, 'Not quite su fast, mi boey; taiak it a bit eeasy.' Ah! twas the ole taiul ovur agen—the old uns a to give in at last to the young uns."

B. "Then you used a faggin-hook in yu-ur time?"

A. "Yis, I a."

B. "But you are not old enough to remember when sickles were used fur reaping?"

A. "Certinly, and I a done it miself many a time when I was a young man; but that was differunt to faggin. We used to ketch holt uv a handful a standin carn, drah the sickul acrass th' alm, and ar-ur a few handfuls were pleeaced togither we tied em up into a sheeaf, so when the shocks were maiad up they stood no higher than the standin alm about em. When the shocks were carried they used to let th' alm stand till it got a few frastes an it, and then men used to goo and beeat it down wi poles, fur then as soon as it was touched it broke awf as brittul as glass. But the best way to saiav laiabur was to drive a flock a ship through the feeuld backurds and forruds. They ood soon fet moast an it down and what was left could very soon be boshed down bi poles. This was called 'baggin th' alm.' The strah was then reeaked up into cocks carrd, and it was the best strah fur thecking. Ah! things be differunt now, what wi machines and self-looaders; why, the ole folks ood die a fright if they could ony rise frum theeur greeavs and see what they be come to now.

"Why, then theeur was 'leeazing.' Neeurly ivverybody in Gahcutt used to goo yeeurs agoo. Theeur were ploughins all ovur the pleeace then. Some an em who had got big families used to git as much carn as ood last em through the gretter part a the wintur. When a feeuld was opun, they used to start arly in the marnin and taiak what food was wanted fur the whool day. They ood kaip in this till it were done ur leeav it as soon as anuther was opuned. That used to be a boon fur many a poour family to git bread in that way; now you nivver see anybody doin it. The peepul thought it a right and that nobody could stop em gooin to leeaz. Sometimes a shock was left standin in the middul a the feeuld and that privented the leeazurs gooin in—that was to say the feeul waunt carrd; but as soon as ivver it was took away, nobody could stop anybody frum gooin in to leeaz. Tha's the law!"

HADDENHAM

(1927)

Interview with Mr. Wm. Plastow

VISITOR. "I have come to ask for a few particulars about the inclosures. I hear you lived soon after they took place, and that you know more about them than anybody living in Haddenham."

MR. PLASTOW. "I waunt alive when that happund; but all I know about em was told me by mi grand-fath-ur. I also heeurd a good many old peepul speeak about em—that was when I was a boey—but they be all dead and gone; none an em be left. They took pleeace in 1831, and I was born in 1839, so I doo-ant remember the opun feeulds and the furlongs; but the incloasures wuz one a the wust things that ivver happund to Hadnum.

"If ye goo along the lower rooad as leeads from Teeam to Aiuhlsburry towards Dintun, ye ull find Hewdon farm layin an the right. Inside one a the barns thaiur's rit an a beeam, 1832—that was the deeat when the incloasures was finished and all the feeulds brought togither into big farms.

"Afuur that the common graiazin land stretched by the streeam frum Dintun to Scotsgrove and then by the side a the river past Notley Abbey, and thaiur all the freeholders had right a pasturige; they were allowed so many cattul aich to graiaze, and if any-body put moour an than what he was allowed, a man who was called a 'driver' druv em awf. He was im-ployed to look arter the cattul, so he knowed how many aich man ought t'ave; but you alwiz find somebody

93

who wants to a moour than his sheear, and that was the way aich man had ony what belonged to him. Well, all the graiazin lands were dividid up into big meddurs, some an em were Stanbridge Meead, Beeany Meead, Middle Meead, Veeasum's Meead, Anxey Meddur, and Youlsome Meead; tuthers I doo-ant remember now. Each a these meeads was sheeard for mowin among different people, but thaiur waunt any hedges, ur balks to mak awf what belonged to aich an em, but what they done was to mark out an the sad an opposit sides a the meead some sign sich as a trough or summut else as ood mark the boundary to ther mowin—one man marked one thing and another another, so they could alwiz tell how fur ther mowin went. The meeads were shet up in spring, and when the grass was fit they employed boeys to run frum one mark athurt the standin grass to the mark an tuther side, and the track the boey maiad showed the boundary a ther mowin; and I a heeurd William Hutt say many a time as he was the boey as run the last path—that was jest afuur th' incloasures took pleeace.

"On Lammas day all the graiazin land become open to the freeholders, so if anybody ant got his hay up by then he ood lose it as all the cattul an that deeat were turned out to pasture, and it waunt alwiz as they got ther hay up by then, fur sometimes thaiur was a wet summur like we a had this yeeur, and then it was a bad thing for many an em.

"The arable land a the parish lay up an the high ground out a the raich a the floods and was dividid into three gret feeulds called Downhill feeuld, Dolli-cott feeuld, and Cott's Hill feeuld, and the three-

course system was alwiz follured. One lay fallur
aich yeeur. Aich a these feeulds was divided up into
smaller ones, and these into the furlongs with the
balks atween. Some a these smaller feeulds had sometimes as many as fifteen or sixteen furlongs and some
had moour, each a th' furlongs was about a
aiacre, but an the whool they used to be a li-ul under.
Some had perhaps forty or fifty a these furlongs,
and they were pleeacd all ovur the parish. Perhaps
thaiur were one or two in one feeuld neeur Dintun,
five or six neeur Notley Abbey, and perhaps twenty
or thurty in other parts a the parish, so it was a bit
inconvainient to cultivaiat, but the people got a good
livin, and they had the reward fur the wurk they
put an the land. The cattul in the summer graiazed
an the fallurs and an the balks, that was when the
meeads were shet up fur mowin. When harvist
come and the craps stood in the feeulds, aich man
had to pay his tenth fur tithe. Thaiur was one
shock in ivvery ten, ivvery tenth cock a barley,
ivvery tenth mule a milk, ivvery tenth pig, and a
tenth of anythink else that was grown an the land,
but they dint taiak ivvery tenth child; I nivver
heeurd as they done that, and thaiur were a good
few an em in Hadnum at that time.

"Well, about 1830 some noatices were put an the
church door, sayin that the feeulds were gooin to be
incloased. When the news got about the village, the
people went and toour [tore] em down. They were
put up agen, but they toour em down agen, but it
waunt no use, fur the Commissionur come down and
started to incloase the feeulds. Thaiur was one man
who had moour to do wi it than anybody else, as

95

he stood to gaian a good deeul; but it waunt long afure he had a terrible affliction, and the people all su-ur it was judgmint an him. Poor thing, his dartur was helpliss all hur life, and she ant bin long dead; but we maunt judge nobody.

"Howivver, when the Commissionur startid, they were sich a long time befuur anythink was done that fur a whool yeeur the people dint know in what parts of the parish the land allottid to em was pleeaced; so that yeeur nauthing was sowed and nobody had any craps at the eend an it; neeurly ivvery small man was practically ruined. Nauthing had come in, and thaiur was the ixpense of ther families gooin an all the time. Next yeeur when they had got thaiur land, thaiur was the ixpense of quickin and incloasin it, fur the Commissionur woont give a proper titul to the incloasure if it waunt in order. An the top a this, new rooads had to be maiad and the ixpense a these all come out a the reeats, so they riz to ovur a pound in the pound. The little man coont feeace this, and so most an em went to the wall, bisides if he had any cattul he coont graiaze em now an the commun feeulds, so he found neeurly all was gone. Some took mortgages an ther land, but coont pay the interest and were sold out, and a few yeeurs laiater the price a carn fell, and most a them who had strugguld to kaip an could kaip an no longer, and they fell out too. Some yeeurs artur the carn riz, and the few as had got ovur the terrible times got an and maiad therselves.

"These times lasted fur some yeeurs, and then come the opportunity for rich men to taiak advantage of the poour. They bought the small farms and added

em to theirn, and ony imployed as many men an the
whool lot as could cultivaiat one farm propurly. I
heeurd one man say, 'When ye see feeuld added to
feeuld an farm to farm, then it's bad fur the whool
village,' and so it was, ispecially fur Hadnum, and I
hope sich a time ull nivver come agen.

"It was a cryin shaiam for the hard-wurkin man to
lose his land and become a laiabourer, and Hadnum
was full an em artur the incloasures. Afuur thaiur
were moour shephurds in the village than what thaiur
are farm laiabourers at the present day. Nobody ood
lend the poour man any money to help him; then
if he kep his land, how could he buy stock to dress
it. Ivverything was agenst him, but it waunt agenst
the man wi plenty a money. I knowed one man wi
plenty who had a ai-acre a turnups, gret turnups as
ivver I did see. He went to Aiuhlsburry markut
and bought forty good strong ship and folded em an
the feeuld. In a week he sold em fur ten shillings a
piece more than what he gin fur em, bisides thaiur
was another crap next year when he sowed his carn;
but how could a poour man do that? He ant got
the money to buy the ship and nobody ood lend it
him. The pleeace was filled with laiabourers and
they dint know wheeur to git a job. Some an em
used to walk to Dintun to git a day's threshin, but
if it raiand they got no money, and yit afuur the
incloasures they had had ther own land. Then they
did git summut fur ther laiabour, fur whativver they
put in the land they got out an it and moour too,
fur they did wurk hard and got a reward fur what
they done. The schooulmaster at Dintun used to
come ovur and spaik to the men, and then they got

Joseph Arch down, and as times dint seem to improve, a good many men, and thauir were some fine strong men in Hadnum then, left the village; some went to Lancashire and Yorkshire, bisides other pleeaces, and some went abroad."

VISITOR. "The saiam ole taiul, the fine ole stock of Englishmen druv out a the country."

MR. PLASTOW. "Well, ivverybody waunt down an em. Thaiur was ole Squire Franklin as did ivverything he could to help em as rentid lands awf him. He gin em stock and in some ceeases [cases] woont taiak any rent fur three yeeurs. If thaiur had bin moour men like him, Hadnum woont a suffered as it did."

VISITOR. "How did all these unemployed men with their families live?"

MR. PLASTOW. "They dint know what to do; they sarched ivverywhere fur imploymint, but few could git it; thaiur was gret distress and want all through the pleeace. The wust an it was thaiur waunt any allotments then; they come laiater. Some a the housen had a few pole a ground at ther back duur, but not enoh to lay by a stooar a taiaturs fur the wintur; besides, taiaturs were sceearce in them days. Some a the farmers let ther men a ten or twenty poles a ground in one a ther feeulds, and that was how they eeked out a livin; but them as were out a wurk dint a that; they had to goo wi-out, and it was ispecially bad fur em when thaiur was a hard winter. Nobody can realise what a blessing it is to have a good crap a taiaturs stoared in yur barn fur the winter, ony them as a bin through hard times like they were in Hadnum artur the incloasures. When ye got em in yur barn they be yourn, and ye can goo and git

em whenivver ye want em. The peepul used to a
pais cooked wi whativver they got and they also used
to a pai-soup. The farmers then growed a lot of
pais, and they used to be sold in the shops. I a took
many a looad to Aiuhlsbury to be sold in the shops.
Ivverybody used to have em. When autumn come,
the big cabbage as were grown in the garduns were
liftid up by the roots and tied head downurds under
the roof a the barn with the dirt an. Then in wintur
ye used to goo and cut a bit out, jest as much as ivver
ye wantid. Thaiur waunt much fresh mait fur the
poour, but they had baiacon dumpling sometimes."

VISITOR. "I know it. I a had some in mi time."

MR. PLASTOW. "A long su-ut puddun wi chopped
baiacon in it mixed up wi inen. When I went to
the schooul jest behind the Wesleyan Chapul, thaiur
was a boey as alwiz brought a inen dumpling fur
dinner; that was a big inen biled in the dumpling—
some used to a them. Times be better now, and a
good thing they be. I a bin a-reeadin in the paiaper
as they be puttin up new housen with ony ten pole a
gardun ground. That's wrong. Ivvery new house
ought to a a a rood a ground, then a man can git enoh
to last him and his family all the yeeur round, bisides
havin summut as he can sell. If at the time a the
incloasures the people a Hadnum had a rood or so
as they could a cultivaiated, thaiur woont a bin the
distress as thaiur wur; twur the delay a the Commissionur's in not tellin the people fur a whool yeeur
wheeur ther lands lay as maiad Hadnum goo to the
wall.

"Ah, I lived wi mi ole grandfath-ur and grand-
moth-ur. I knowed what they had suffered, and

since they a bin dead, I a laid abed many a time and cried at what they went through. They a bin at rest now fur a good long while, and it wunt be long afuur I be at rest wi em, as I be eighty-seven yeeurs old and can't ixpect to live much longer. Ah! many a time in the long dark nights have I thought an em and what they done fur me; and then I think a mi past life and what I a done. Sometimes I graive and sometimes I feeul happy.

"Well, my boey, alwiz do what's right, and if ye can help it nivver do any wrong. If ye cant do nobody any good, nivver do em any harm, fur tis them people as do harm as alwiz causes sich misery in the woruld. Thaiur's one thing I always feeul I done right in, and I awfen think an it. My grand-moth-ur had brought me up from a baiaby and ceeard [cared] fur me like a mothur. They alwiz looked artur me and sheeuldid me and protectid me quite as much as if she had bin mi own peearent [parent]. When I had got to be a strongish lad, I begun to think a what e was gooin to be, and I thought e would be a carpinter, fur I dint like the idea of havin to goo through what they had gone through; so I used to tell it about pritty awfen, not knowin I should a to leeav the village to git apprenticed. One day, when induurs, I mentioned it agen, and I could see by ther feeaces they were a bit concarned. So one day soon artur she says to me, 'When yur poour mothur died and left ye a baiaby, we took ye, and brought ye up and a alwiz a-treeated ye as ur own child. We a looked artur ye and ceeared for ye, and now we be a-gittin old and can't wurk, we thought ye ood stay wi us and help us in ur old age.

Ye ull do wrong if ye leeav us.' All at once I
thought a the sacrifice they had maiad for me all
through the terrible time they had pahst, so I said,
'Granny, I ull nivver leeav ye nur fursaiak ye as long
as ivver ye live.' And I nivver did. I lived wi em
all ther lives and helped em all I could till they boath
died, and then I laiad em to rest."

VISITOR. "When did they die?"

MR. PLASTOW. "My grandfath-ur died in 1865
and my grandmoth-ur a few yeeurs afuur that. I
alwiz feel I done right in stayin wi em, and that a
bin one a the grettest satisfactions a mi life. My
grandfath-ur left me the little house we lived in and
about a ai-acre a ground to 't, but it was mortgaged
fur moour than it was wuth. At the time a the
incloasures he got about twenty ai-acres at Roundhill
fur his lot. He kep sixteen and sold tuthers to pay
his debts; but the reeats fur the new rooads and the
ixpenses a quickin and incloasin were too much fur
him, and he coont git an. Th' overseers were
always a-callin fur money; thaiur was one ooman
who was afreead whenivver she heeurd her frunt
geeat opun as she thought somebody was shuur to
come fur money; she toald me that hurself. Why,
they coont pay sometimes the rooadman ther weekly
waiages a aiaht shillings a week; they had to goo to
somebody to git him to pay his reeats an the Saturday
afuur the man could be paid—thaiur waunt no money
about.

"My grandfath-ur had a lot a bad luck at that time.
He had a cow die and then a horse; so he sold one
horse fur sixty pounds and put it in the bank, and
another to a man fur the saiam money, but he nivver

paid fur it. Soon arter the bank broke and he only got sixty half-crowns fur his sheear. So one thing comin an the top a tuther broke him and he had to give up. He got a man naimd Cross a London to buy his sixteen aiacres fur twenty-two pounds a aiacre, but neeurly all an it went in the reeats and ixpenses a encloasin. At the saiam time the man agreed to let my grandfath-ur have a leeas an the land at twenty-two shillins a aiacre fur twenty-one yeeurs. As soon as the man got it he took part an it away and planted it wi trees, then he took some moour and at last all an it; and that's how my grand-fath-ur was left wi ony the little cottage wi the one aiacre attached to it.

"Ah! these men frum London as lent money an mortgage were a hard lot—they had no murcy an the poour. They got ivverything they could and took ivvery advantage, so that whoivver got in ther hands was stripped of all he got. This is the kind a men they were: Some Hadnum men borrowed some money frum one a these London men, and soon they begun to feel his tarms were a bit hard; so they went up to London to see if they could git a bit awf. They went to his shop, and when they went inside he was in it among his wurkpeople. As soon as he see the Hadnum men, he said to them around him, 'You a got some funny fellurs heeur, but I ull show ye summut wonderful.'

"He then went to speeak to the Hadnum men and said, 'I sell ivverything in my shop. I can let ye have whativver ye want.' So one an em said, 'Then sell me a bit a barley straa fur mi shoes.' That done him, fur he ant got any a that. Soon artur he says,

'Heeur's a shilling fur aich an ye.' So he give aich
an em a shilling. 'Now,' says he, 'I a gin aich an ye
a shilling; if ye gi me back the shilling I can gi aich
an ye a half a crown.' So they give him back the
shilling, but he dint give em the half a crown; so
they axed him for it. 'No,' says he, 'I dint say as I
ood gi it ye back, I said I *could*; but I baint a gooin
to.' So they had nauthing at all. That was the kind
a men the people had to deeul wi in them days.

"Well, my grandfath-ur was left at last wi ony
his little cottage and a aiacre a ground, and artur his
death I got married and lived in it. I wurked as
hard as any man did (and I could wurk in them
days). I wurked forrad in the marnin and laiat at
night, but e coont git an as the interest e had to pay
an the mortgage swallured ivverything e arnt. One
night a fire broke out in th' house and burnt it to the
ground. We escaiaped [escaped] wi our lives, but
lost ivverything ixcept a few things. The naiahbours
were good; they took us in and sheltered us, and gin
mi childern some clo-athes. I got a hunderd pounds
frum the insurance, so I paid it to the man who hilt
the mortgage, and then was left wi nauthing.

"Howivver, I found e was better off wi ony mi
weekly waiages at twelve shilling a week, fur now
e ant got any moour interest to pay; and so e went
an. I come in this heeur house arter the fire and I
be in it now. Ah! I wurked hard to maiak eends
meet—and I a wurked hard in mi time. I a fagged
half a aiacre a day many a time and arned me five
shillings—I was at it at fuur o'clock in the marnin
till laiat at night. I wurked fur mi mahster fur
thurty yeeurs, and alwiz sarved him faithfully. I

alwiz done ivverything e could and done the very
best fur him. He was a man wi plenty a money.
He done his land well, so he had good returns. His
yard were alwiz full a stock—ivvery carner an it—
and his barns were alwiz full a graian [grain]. He
done his feeulds well, fur his yard wuz alwiz full a
dung. He trusted me wi the kays a the grinnery,
and I was risponsible fur ivverything as was stooard
thaiur.

"Well, a married son lived wi him, and a relation
a the son's wife come to live wi em. He was a
butcher by traiad, but ant got an very well; but
he used to kill a ship occasionally and goo round the
district and sell the mait: sometimes he used to goo
to Teeam markut.

"Well, my mahster always trusted me, and I used
to put the kays a the grinnery in a sartin pleeace.
When I was in the cowhus, I sometimes see him a-
meddlin about wi the kays and sometimes a-comin
out a the grinnery with summut in a bag. When I
went to look at what was happenin, I could see
hooals in the heeaps a graian—and big hooals, too—
so I maiad up mi mind to cleeur miself, fur if e dint,
e should git miself shet up in Aiuhlsburry fur no
fault a mi own, and very likely git transported. The
moour I thought an it the gretter the deeanger I
could see e was in. When it was found out, as it
soon would a bin, as ivvery bushul as went in had
bin booked, they ood a took no noatice a what I had
to say, and if I had then tried to put it an the right
person they ood a said, 'Why dint you tell us an it
befuur?' I felt I was in danger a losing mi good
naiam and being thought a thaif as long as ivver e

lived. So I maiad up mi mind to tell ivverything. I went home and told mi wife what e was a-gooing to do, and she agreed wi me.

"Fur the next few days I coont see mi mahster, as he was ill; but when he come downsteears and got about, and I run agen him the fust time, I said, 'Master, I be gooin to tell ye summat's happenin with the carn in the grinnery': so I toald him all. When I had done, I said, 'Now I know I shall a to goo fur it. Mrs. —— ull be shuur to git me the sack.' 'No,' says he, 'I ull see to that.' Howivver, it waunt long artur when I was a-milkin in the cowhus, when she comes in and says, 'Will-yum, come and do the churmin!' I said, 'I ull as soon as I a maiad the cows all saiaf.' She says, 'You wunt do as ye are toald'; so I said, 'I ull come as soon as ivver I can, but I must tie the cows up saiafly.' I done this as soon as ivver e could, and then went and done the churmin; then I went back to the cowhus and finished mi milkin. 'Ah!' I thought, 'she a got me now.'

"Soon artur mi mahster come hooam, and in a little while he walked acrass to me and said, 'Will-yum, I heeur as ye woont do as ye were toald.' I says, 'Master, I coont leeav the cows till I had maiad all saiaf.' He says, 'Heeur's yur waik's money and goo at once.' 'No, master,' says I, 'I shant; you ull a to gi mc another waik's pay in lieu a noatice.' He says, 'I shant; you ant done as you were toald, so you ull a to goo at once.' 'Then,' says I, 'I shant leeav the pleeace until I git the two waiks' pay,' and he had to gi it me; so I got the two waiks' waiages and left.

"When I got hooam and toald mi wife, she says, 'You ull git wurk somewheeur else. Dooant wurry.

Summut ull be shuur to come along,' and it did soon
arter. Well, I nivver bore em any malice, fur that
would a bin a wrong thing to do, and it waunt very
long afuur a relation a theirn axed me to wurk fur
him, but I dint goo, as I had got a very good pleeace
in the farm not very fur away. Howivver, I used
to help em in my speear time, ispecially when they
wer busy.

"One aivening a beautiful horse a theirn fell back
wi the strangles, so they fot me and I did what e
could, and at last got the horse round. Mi old
mahster, when he see the horse was better, said to
me, 'Will-yum, you shull a a good suppur to-night,
and a pint a beeur and as many moour as ye can
drink.' When the wurk was done I went in his
kitchen wi him, and he went through into tuther
rooms and toald em what to do. I sot down in a
cheear and waiated fur the suppur, and thaiur I sot
till I almost went to slaip. Nauthing come in.

"Arter a time he comes in and says, 'Will-yum, I
hope you a injoyed yur suppur!' 'Thenkee,' says I,
'I ant had naiur a bit a nauthing to ett, and naiur a
drap a beeur to drink.' 'You ant!' says he. 'No,'
says I, 'I ant.' 'Well,' says he, 'I ull goo and see to
that.' He went in tuther room, and I heeurd him
say to the son's wife who had got me the bag, 'How's
this? I toald you to gi Will-yum a good suppur,
and as much beeur as he could drink, and you ant
done it. You ee-ant mahster in this house yit, and
you wunt be while I be alive. Goo and git him
summut to ett and some beeur to drink at once.'

"Soon arter she brought a nice bit a baif in and
some beeur and throwed it down at me as if she

had bin a-faiding the pigs; but I dint mind that. I set to and had a good suppur wi plenty a beeur, and when I had had enoh I went hooam to bed.

"I knowed he was alwiz sorry fur gitting rid a me, and I alwiz felt I could a gone back whenivver I liked, but I dint goo. He was a good farmer, and if ivvery farmer done his land as he done his, it ood be a good thing fur ivverybody. I had no regrets, fur I alwiz sarved him faithfully. Many a time did I goo back an dark winter nights artur supper to see if all was well in the staiables and cowhus, fur sometimes a cow or a horse gits loose and then damage is done.

"Ye can't realise what harm is done when the cattul beeant tied up saiafly—ony them as a sin it know what happuns. Sometimes one ull slip its cheean an then goo a-wanderin about among tuthers all night, an then thaiur's shuur to be trouble afu-ur the marnin; an ye neeurly alwiz find the master-cow is the one as gits loose, an that's the one as is shu-ur to do moast damage."

(His daughter leaves the room.)

"That's mi dahter. She was in sarvice in London when mi poo-ur wife died. She was in a good pleeace, but she left it an come hooam to look artur me. If she ant a done I dunno what e should a done; I be affeard e should a to a gone to the Dumplin House. Howivver, she come an looked arter me ivver since, an I deearsay she ull to the eend."

VISITOR. "She ull git hur reward some day."

MR. PLASTOW. "Well, I a now bin three yeeurs dooin nauthin. I had the rheumatics come an me an e was obliged to give up—an heeur e be, can't do much, ony do mi gardun an a few odd jobs about th' ouse; an yit e could do a good day's wurk if they ood ony leeav me. I feeul as healthy as e did yeeurs agoo, an can injoy mi meeuls as much as ivver e did, but e can't git about, e be so crippuld. I be ai-ahty-seven now, an a outlived ivverybody older than miself as e knowed when e was a boey: I feeul thankful that e a bin presarved an bin in good health all mi life. Sometimes when I be a-sittin heeur alooan, I think uv the ole feeaces as a gone, and then the blessins I a recaived through mi long life crap up in mi mind. The time seems pritty long some days, but I do a littul reeading, an that teeaks the dullniss awf. Ivvery marnin I reead two a the Psalms, an I do the saiam ivvery night; an I awfen reead some pree-ars, an they cumfurt me, but I do miss not bein able to goo to church an a Sunday. I should so like to goo to the pleeace wheeur God's neeam is honoured, an wheeur His peepul assemble, but e can't, as tis too fur away, an e can't walk. Howivver, I hope e shull some day, as I be havin a littul cheear an wheeuls maiad at the blacksmith's, so as e can wheeul miself down thaiur bi turnin th' handuls as I sit in the sait. I a got some money seeavd bi me to pay for 't and e be a seeavin what e can. If e could git down to sarvice ivvery Sunday, thaiur ood be summut to look forrad to, an the time woont hang so heavy as it do some-times."

VISITOR. "I hope it will soon be ready for you."

MR. PLASTOW. "I shull git it soon, but e can't seeav much a week, as e ony got the Old Ai-age Pen-sion to live an."

VISITOR. "Well, I should like to see ivvery farmur's man who a wurked hard all his life have ivvery cumfurt he wants when he gits an in life."

MR. PLASTOW. "An they desarve it, fur thaiur's no class a men moour desarvin than what they be. They be up arly in the marnin, an they wurk laiat at night, an when they a wurked hard all ther lives they ought not to a the wurkhus a-steearin em in the feeace when they git too old fur work. When ye a got good, honist, straiaht-forrud, hard-workin laiabourers, they should a some reward. Nobody can tell the value uv a good laiabourer, whether he's a cattulman, shephurd, ur laiabourer. Ivvery one an em knows exactly what to do, an when tis done, the mahster knows its well done. You can't tell the value uv a good farm laiabourer to his mahster, an yit nobody thinks nauthin an him; he's the wust paid uv all an yit what would the country do wiout him? When ye git good mahsters an good laiabourers, ivverything goos an well. Thaiur's alwiz plenty a stock an the farm, plenty a laiabour, an plenty a dress an the land; then ye git plentiful craps. Uv cu-urse if the saison's bad you git some spoilt, but teeakin it an the whool, thaiur's plenty, an that's what we want right through the country. I know ye git bad mahsters as well as bad laiabourers—mahsters who ant got the money to treeat the soil as it should be treeated, an think they ull git out what they ant put in."

(Conversation is interrupted and resumed.)

MR. PLASTOW. "Ah! I was a-speeakin about bad cultivaiation. You git some farmers who add feeuld to feeuld and farm to farm, an ony imploy an em all as many as could ony propurly cultivaiat one farm. Then ye see the land niglected and not half done. Thaiur ant the laiabour to cleean it, and very soon the feeulds git covered wi waids and rubbish. Ye must a plenty a cattul in yur yard to put back an the land what ye a took frum it. If ye faid the land it ull faid you. Ye a got to treeat it like ye treeat anythink else, and then ye ull git yur returns. If ye starve it yeeur by yeeur and let it git overrun wi waids and rubbish, then ye git very little increeas— not much moour than what ye a put in; but dress it well and kaip it cleean, then ye git the increeas. When I had pigs in mi sty, I used to put the pig-dung round the roots a the bushes in mi gardun, and I had currunts as big as churries, and goosburries as big as warnuts, and its jest like this in the ceeas a ivvery-thing as grows an the land—it must a food to do its wurk.

"Some people think they can git summut out a nauthing—but they cant, and nivver wull. All mi life I a noaticed that land wi no dress gis very poour craps—short straa, little eeurs, and little kurnuls; but land well dressed always gis good craps—long straa, long eeurs, and big kurnuls; and I nivver yit sin big eeurs wi fat kurnuls an thin short straa, and nobody else nivver did. When carn is sold by weight, ant it better to taiak a peck out a the sack, than put a peck in? That's the difference atween good and bad farmin. You must a cleean land, plenty a dress, and plenty a laiabour to git th' increeas, and when ye a got these, the increeas comes. And what cleeans the land like a good ploughsheear! How it turns the ground ovur and distroys all the rubbish,

ispecially when ye a got a good man behind the
plough. I a bin a-reeadin out a the 'Ole Book' jest
afuur you come in, and it says the 'time ull come
when all the su-urds and speears shull be turned into
ploughsheears and pruning hooks.' Then all the
docks and the curlook and the cockuls and the thissuls
and the nettuls and ivvery other kind a rubbish ull
be distroyed. Then THE LAND ULL BE CLEEAN, and
not only that, all malice and haiatred and covetous-
ness ull be driven frum men's hearts. That ull be a
happy time fur ivverybody, and it ull be shu-ur to
come—the 'Ole Book' says so—but I shant live to see
it. Ah! that wull be a blessed time! Thaiur ull be
good mahsters ivverywheeur wi plenty a laiabour an
the farm. The laiabourers ull git good waiages while
the mahster gits the increeas. His yard ull be full
a stock—ivvery carner an it—and his grinneries full
a graian. His feeulds, ivvery one an em, ull be well
dressed, fur he's got plenty a dung; then thaiur ull
be plenty fur ivverybody, fur the increeas is shuur
to follur.

"Wurkin an the land is lovely wurk—and in mi
time I wurked fu-urteen and fifteen hours a day, but
that was afuur the machines come about. We sowed
by hand, ripped by hand, and threshed wi the thraiul.
It was lovely wurk, and that was how it was done
when I was a young man. We used to dibble the
sayd in, and I a dibbled many a aiacre a wheeat,
beeans, wuts, and barley. Sometimes we used to sow
broadcast. At harvist we cut wi a sickle. We took
a handful a carn and cut it, leeavin about a foot a
halm standin, so then the sheeavs waunt very big and
easily dried. When the sheeavs were stored in the

barn, it was most carn and a lot could be put in. Arterwards we cut the standin halm and mixed it wi the cowdung, as that was the toughest, the tuther holdin the corn was gin to the cattle as food.

"When threshin-time come we used to thresh wi a thraiul, and this was the very best way too. The chaff is swaiter, and the kurnuls a corn are not so much damaged as when they goo through the brushes of a threshin machine. Thaiur waunt a speck a dust an the threshin-fluur when we used the thrail, and many a time we threshed clover an it. Ivverything was swait and nice—different to what tis at the present day. Ah! tis lovely wurk, and if I had mi time ovur agen, I ud goo an the land. Some peepul be shet up all day in offices and factories and nivver have any fresh air—and this ant no good to em; but when ye wurk an the land ye are in the fresh air all the time. Ye see the land ploughed an harrud, the sayd put in, and then ther growth. At harvist time ye see all round ye the results a yer laiabour. It is lovely wurk, and if I had mi time ovur agen, and I was a boey a ten yeeurs a age, I ud goo streeaht to a farm and git imployed. Yis, I ood.

I ood plough and sow,

(*after a pause*)

And raip and mow,
And be a farmer's boy."

(*The old gentleman looked up and smiled*)

VISITOR. "That's the one! We can't beat it!"
MR. PLASTOW. "Yis, I ood; and I alwiz be glad I went an the land. I know when e lived wi mi old

grandfath-ur e wanted to be a carpinter, but now I be thankful e nivver went."

VISITOR. "Well, tis gittin an, and I shull a to be a-gooin."

MR. PLASTOW. "Well, taiak a few beeans and taiators in yur pockut wi ye. Ye be welcome."

VISITOR. "I know e be; I ull. I nivver say 'No' to a broad beean."

MR. PLASTOW. "Have as many as ye like."

VISITOR. "Thenks."

MR. PLASTOW. "A ye got enoh?"

VISITOR. "Plenty; I shall cook em tomorra and I know I shall injoy em."

MR. PLASTOW. "Thaiur's nauthing like having a good appetite. I can ett a meeul a vittles as well as ivver e did in all mi life, though I be eighty-seven yeeurs old."

VISITOR. "Well, good night. I ull call agen, and have a talk on the incloasures."

MR. PLASTOW. "Yis, do: I shall be glad to se ye any time, and tell ye what I know about em. Good night."

STOKENCHURCH

Casual Conversation in a Cosy Tap-room

A (Old man sitting in corner). "Shet that du-ur! The draught's enough to cut ye a-two. I git sick and tired an it. Nobody thinks a shettin the du-ur when they goo out. Thaiur e be as soon as tis opun, sittin streeaht in the draught. Ivvery night tis jest the saiam, no mah-hur whehur they be gooin fur good ur comin back agen, they alwiz leeav it opun. Tis about time some an em thought a somebody else."

B. "Wha's the mah-hur?"

A (angrily). "Why, left the du-ur opun agen and the draught's enough to blow anybody away. Tis about time when some an ye leeav the room as ye should larn to shet the du-ur."

(Silence for a short time.)

DOMINO PLAYERS. "Ah! Ah! Ah! got him! E wuz a-waiatin fur ye! Ye coont help yurself! E thought e should a ye! E was a-waiatin. E thought he was a-comin! A good gaiam! A very good gaiam! Shufful! Now then, goo an! Fu-ur and five maiaks nine! Do what ye can wi that. Plai-ah. Goo an. I ull plai-ah two—a double one, I meean. Good! Tha's a good un! Well plai-ahd! Another ai-ahpunny gone! Peg me ai-aht! A purty three, pardner! No, I ant got no three. Fet me a pint. Fill mine up! Ye beeant a-peggin right! Ye be a-peggin backurds! A gurt one. A gurt one! Domino an one! Teeak it. Hold an a second! Purty! Purty! Purty! Be doin well to-night! Coont git an at all last night! Domino! A ye took it! No? Well, taiak it then!"

A. "Good aivenin, Chawley! How is it outside?"

B. "A bit dark and jest a reeanin a li-ul: it saims as if it's a-gooin to kaip an."

A. "Dooant sit thaiur; the draught's enough to blow ye away when they opun the du-ur." (*Sits down.*) "I had a walk down the rooad this marnin and called in at the Reeaven fur a li-ul while, but dint see anybody down thaiur."

B. "I see ole Jim a-carrin the pleeats wi his ai-apurn an."

A. "Well, as I was a-gooin down I met ole —— a-comin up. He was a-weearin that big cooat a hisn and it looked all right too. When he come out a th' army they gin him a chance to buy it—he had aither to pay a sovereign fur it ur send it back; so he paiad the money and had it dyed. I rickun he's got a good bargin. Tis one a them ovurcooats as all the sojurs had fur wintur."

A. "How be ye awf fur wurk?"

B. "Jest gooin gently an! Ant got much to spaik an."

(Silence for some short time.)

C. "How long is it agoo since Tom Sayers treeand up heeur at Sto-aken?"

A. "When he fout Heenan?"

B. "Ah, that was the time."

A. "Why, about sixty ur seventy eeur agoo. I cant rimembur much an it, but I a heeurd th' ole folks spaik a good deeul about it."

C. "It was a bit lively up heeur then, waunt it?"

A. "No mistaiak about that, fur the young fellurs frum all ovur the pleeace used to come up and try to git a round wi him, but twaunt no good, fur he knocked em about like ninepins. When he was in treeanin he used ivvery marnin to run down the meddurs as fast as ivver he could, and then come back and git in the blankuts. That maiad him sweat like a horse and tha's how he kep his wai-aht down."

C. "He got a bit a pluck in him."

A. "He had; and thaiur's no mistaiak about that, to fight su many rounds ah-ur he broke his arm."

C. "How did that happun?"

A. "Why, Heenan hit him an th' arm and broke it, and he fout fifteen ur sixteen rounds wi ony one arm."

C. "How did it eend?"

A. "Why, the crowd rushed the ring and endid the fight. If Tom could a had the use a boath his arms, thaiur's no doubt he would a won; as it was, Heenan coont see fur waiks ar-urwurds."

C. "I suppooas you do a bit a that up heeur now?"

A. "Not much now; but thaiur used to be a good deeul an it done once an a time, ispecially at the Feear."

C. "I a heeurd thaiur was, but I suppooas most a th' old uns be gone."

A. "They be; they be neeurly all gone."

C. "Is Alfred Witney dead?"

A. "Ees."

C. "I heeurd Will-yum Grimsdull died eeurs agoo."

A. "Ah! some time now."

C. "I suppooase ole Dodgur is too?"

A. "Ees."

C. "Is ole Pimmock Bird still alive?"

A. "No, he's dead."

C. "Did ye ivver see sich a cock as he was? I niver did see a cock like him!"

A. "And nobody else nivver did!"

C. "We shull nivver see the likes an him agen."

A. "We nivver sholl. O rimembur him well, a-gooin to Wycombe mo-ast days a the waik wi his donkey-cart full a chips and sheeavins, and ole Hannur [Hannah] a-trudgin bi his side ur jest ah-ur him. He was one a the best-hearted fellurs as ivver lived, fur thaiur's one thing he alwiz done, and tha's what nobody ood ivver dreeam a dooin now-a-deeas. When he had a pint he alwiz gin his donkey a drap, and very awfen the fust drink. Ah! I can see him now a-swiggin out uv a pint cup, and thaiur's no mistaiak he did injoy it. One day they stopped at the Black Boy, West Wycombe; he alwiz called thaiur whethur he was a-gooin ur comin back. Pimmock called fur his pint as usual and let the donkey have fust drink, but jest a that minute he started talkin to somebody and kep an tippin the cup up, so the ole donkey drunk it all in one draught. As soon as the donkey took his mouth away ole Pimmock see all his beeur gone, so he sez, 'You ole hog; you a bin and drinked all mi beeur and ant left me a drap! You be the biggist hog as ivver I did see!' Howivver, he called fur another pint, and be blowed if he dint let the donkey taiak the top awf a that too."

C. "He was a fine ole fellur. Tis a pity thaiur aint a few moour about like him and all the old uns as used to be up heeur."

A. "'Tis; but thaiur's nobody a-comin an to taiak ther pleeaces."

(*The conversation ceased for a time. During the lull a customer got up and left the door of the tap-room open.*)

A. "Shet that du-ur! Left it opun agen! I be sick a-hollurin! I nivver did see sich a lot!"

(*On the customer's return the game of dominoes started again.*)

DOMINO PLAYERS. "Another gaiam! Saiam pard-ners! Cam an! You call t' me! Odd! Tha's aiven! Waiat a jiffy! Fet me a pint a my-ul [mild] afuur us starts. Fi-ull mine! I ull a alf a one! Ready! Goo an! Gi White a down! I dunno as I can goo. Thaiur ye be, fur one! Taiak us two! Can't goo! Taiak us two chalks! Well, e a ony plaiahd two as yet. Cam an, this gaiam ull taiak as long as a crickut-match! Whosen turn? Why, yourn! Why dooant ye look ah-ur the gaiam instid a waiasting time, then we could git an! Purty! A purty three! Ye cant plaiah dominoes and talk at the saiam time. Look ah-ur yur oan affeears and leeav me to look ah-ur mine. Taiak us fuur. Hi! Hi! Hi! Got him! Tha's purty good, pardner! I dint think as ye had got that! What to plaiah! Sixes! Ant got one. Goo an! Cant goo! Taiak us ai-aht and one fur domino—nine! They dint git in the saiam streeat as us! They cant plaiah dominoes. Yu-ur leead! Shant goo! Tha's it, is it? How's that! A gurt one! A gurt one! Taiak me one and anothur fur domino! Gaiam! I a finished!"

(*The conversation is resumed.*)

c. "How be Stokenchurch a-gittin an wi futball this yeeur?"

a. "I belaive they be a-gittin an purty well; they aint lost many gaiams yit—they a won mo-ast an em. Do you teeak any interest in it?"

c. "Not much; e used to once an a time, but e be gittin oldur and tha's out a my line now. I like to see a good gaiam, but ye dooant see em about heeur."

a. "I belaive e a sin yur feeace afuur."

c. "Very likely. I a bin about these parts awf and an all mi life."

a. "Did you use to plai-ah crickuts?"

c. "I did, and up heeur at Stokenchurch yeeurs agoo."

a. "I thought e had plai-ahd agen ye. I saim to remembur yur feeace. Did ye know ole Ted Baiats?" [Bates].

c. "No; he was jest a li-ul afuur my time."

a. "Ah! we had a good teeam up heeur then."

c. "I know ye did."

a. "Did ye know ole Fred Leeacy?" [Lacey].

c. "E should think e did! He alwiz plai-ahd fur West Wycombe. He was a underhand bowel-er and alwiz streeaht an the wickut, and I a heeurd him say many a time that if anybody dint stop one uv his bowels he ood be shuur to heeur a li-ul click behind his bat."

a. "He was a good bowel-er. I plaiahd agen him when we took a teeam down to Fillingdun and plaiahd in the meddur thaiur. Ole Darkie Smith was an ther side."

c. "He was a good un. He larnt his crickuts an West Wycombe hill, and yeeurs agoo a good many

119

crickuturs were turned out thaiur. West Wycombe had a good teeam then."

A. "They did."

C. "Jim Langley frum Downley used to plaiah fur em."

A. "I a heeurd peepul say he was one a the best crickuturs fur myulls around in his day."

C. "He was. He plaiahd ole Tom Smith frum Lewknur fur half a guinea an the frunt a th' ill, and ole Tom used to git hundcrds—that was ar-ur a match."

A. "How did it eend?"

C. "Why, a drah; naiur a one an em could git the tuther out."

A. "I plaiahd agen ole Fred one day in Cofurnul and he kep an puttin his underhand bowels to the leg. At last he pitched one up streeaht at mi head and e missed it. It hit me plump an the jah and neeurly knocked me ovur. I shull nivver furgit ole Fred Leeacy."

C. "Radnidge used to have a good teeam."

A. "They did, but that was some yeeurs leeater. They had as purty a teeam as any villidge could wish t' have. Ivvery man wore the ole red, white, and blue cap wi a tossel."

C. "Tha's it."

A. "They had some good men."

C. "And they ought to, fur when they plaiahed an the Common it waunt like they plaiah now. When anybody went in to bat, he stuck thaiur ti-ull he was got out. That maiad good crickuturs an em; and anothur thing, the scouts dint dawdull when they had to fet a ball. They run fur all they were wuth.

Ye dooant see that now—ivverybody wants to bat ur bowel; they be too idul to run ar-ur any ball. Who used to be in the teeam?"

A. "Why, thaiur were Jack Stooan, Bill Stooan, George Stooan, Jack White, Joe Bowdun, Shinur, Jim Stooan, Tommy Atkins, but e dooant rimember tuthers. I know they could a got a teeam a Stooans, if they had a liked."

C. "Gaw! and dint they sing that ole crickut song a theirn: 'Come, all ye jolly crickuturs'!"

A. "They did; I heeurd em sing it many a time; and they dint half furgit to sing it ispecially when they won."

C. "Do ye know it?"

A. "E used to know it well."

C. "What is it? Let's have it."

A. "E dunno whethur e shall be ai-able to git right through wi it. Here goos."

RADNAGE CRICKET SONG

Come, all ye jolly crickuturs,
    Whoivver ye may be;
I ull a ye pay attention
    And listun anto me.
        Fur to crickuts we wull goo, wull goo,
        To crickuts we wull goo.

We ull goo out an the Common, boys,
    An thaiur we ull choose ur ground;
But fust we ull choose the ompire
    And then we ull choose ur men.
        Fur to crickuts, etc.

Well plaiahd, mi pritty pardner,
 Be shu-ur an bat upright;
An when she comes wi a hop-hop-hop
 We ull cut hur out a sight.
  Fur to crickuts, etc.

Well bowel-d, mi pritty pardner,
 She how she tips the baiul;
An if ye kaip em to that length
 I'm shuur we sholl not faiul.
  Fur to crickuts, etc.

Well throwed, mi pritty pardner,
 She how she nips the wind;
An when she goos bi the bowel-er
 We ull all back up behind.
  Fur to crickuts, etc.

An now the gaiam is endid, boys,
 We ull merrily drink an sing
Good health unto ur crickuturs
 An glory to ur King.
  Fur to crickuts, etc.

An now the gaiam is endid, boys,
 An we a won the ball,
The very nex time we come this way
 We ull gi this house a call.
  Fur to crickuts, etc.

 c. "I remember it well now!"
 a. "They sti-ull sing it!"
 c. "I hope they ull kaip it an fur a good many
yeeurs to come. Who writ it?"

A. "No-body knows, but it's bin sung up in Rad-
nidge as long as ivver I remember and afuur that."
C. "Shoont mind heeurin it agen."
A. "Ah! our crickutin days be ovur."
C. "They be. I shull a to see about gooin. Good
night."

_____

A Cure for the Heartburn

"I was a teetotallur once an a time. I nivver smoked
ur touched a drap a beeur ti-ull e was nineteen, and
e shoont a done then if e ant a suffurd awful wi th'
heartburn, as maiad me as e dint know what to do
wi miself. E was alwiz havin it, day ar-ur day; e
could nuther ett ur drink but what e was alwiz
paiad out for 't. I tried ivverything, but do whativver e could e coont git rid an it.

"Ye know what tis; tis summut as rises in ye and
comes up in yu-ur throoat and burns like a red-hot
iron and then it goos back. It maiaks ye feeul as
miserabul as a dog. Leeat one marnin as e was a-layin
in bed it riz and neeurly stranguld me. I thought e
should a died, as e nivver did a sich a touch.

"Ar-ur it was ovur I laid a li-ul while and then
said to miself, 'I shull a to do summut, fur I can't
stand it any longur.' I jumped out a bed, put mi
clo-athes an, and went downsteears. As soon as I
got down, I see mi fathur, so I said, 'Dad, I be gooin
to a some beeur.' So he says, 'I be very sorry to
heeur ye say so, mi boey; dooant start now.' 'Well,'
I says, 'I a jest bin neeurly stranguld and I a stood
it quite long enough; e must do summut.'

"I put mi hat an and walked acrass the common wheeur they were havin a club-feeast. I went in as bad as ivver e could be, and sot down and had a pint a beeur and a pipe a backur. Ar-ur a few swigs, I felt a bit behher, so when e had finished e had anothur. I soon begun to feeul a bit dizzy, so e went back to bed. I slep like a top, and when e awoke e felt a differunt man. Ivvery day since that time e a alwiz had mi beeur and backur, and streeang to say e a nivver once had th' eartburn. It quite cured me."

WHEELER END

(1927)

A. "Do it reean?"

B. "Tis jest a spettin a little. We shant git none. It's bin like this fur the last three waiks—cloudy and threatenin all day, an then cleeurin auf a nights."

A. "Sombody a had it this arturnoon. The starm seemed to pass ovuur tuther side a Wycombe, but we ony had a few draps heeur—jest the taiul-eend an it."

B. "I heeur they had a good drap at Downley."

A. "Well, I a sin somebody who a bin up thaiur, an they ant had none at all to speeak an, so somebody a bin tellin lies."

B. "Now, we had jest a little to wet ivverything. It ull be a bad thing fur the bloom if it cleeurs up, as we shall be shuur to git a frast if it do; the wind is su cold, it wunt git out a the north. This marnin, when I got up, it lay thick an the grass, but what we a had leeatly a bin white frastes, an they dooant hurt, as ivverything is su dry. Tis them thaiur black frastes as do the damidge when it fraizes the stalks right through, an as soon as the sun comes out maiaks em turn black an drap auf."

A. "Well, what I can see an it, the bloom looks pritty well, ispeshully th' apples, an the churries be all right too. I dooant think they a bin harmed at all—it a bin su dry; but thaiur, if we do git a crap, th' ole blackburds ull have em neeurly all. I a got a nice little orchurd a trees, an as soon as ivver the churries turn colour they be at em. They baint like the threshurs, as alwis stop ti-ull they neeurly git ripe, an a wurkin man like miself can't stop at hooam an look arter em all day long when e a got summut else to do. E nivver did see sech artful burds as the blackburds. They be up afu-ur the sun rises, and the wust an it is they be arly to bed, so when e gits hooam artur wurk they be all at roost. When they come in a tree they alwis have a look roun to see if anybody's about, an if they spy somebody wi a gun they be auf like lightnin afu-ur ye can git a shot. They baint like th' ole threshurs and starlins, as comes in and sticks thaiur; you can fetch them down, but th' ole blackburds be dabsters. I a got a pond in mi orchurd, an in the dry weathur they come up and drink long afu-ur I be up, an then they goo down in the wood an tell tuther burds; so they all come up an spoil no eend a churries long afu-ur I be up an about. Tis no good a-tryin to kaip em away, so I let em alooan, an git jest the few they leeav."

c. "You used to have some good ole kinds grow up heeur. I suppoase ye a got em stiull?"

a. "Oh, ah, we a!"

c. "What's ther naiams?"

a. "Why, Croons, Blackbuds, an Blackhearts; all these be good boath fur ettin and fur pies."

c. "Then ye sti-ull maiak the ole churry pie up heeur?"

a. "Oh, ah; I should think we do."

c. "These be the churries as maiaks yu-ur mouth black when ye ett the pies."

a. "Oh, ah; they be; twoont be a propur churry pie if it dint maiak yu-ur mouth black when ye wur ettin it. They a all got a nice bit a flesh an em, an the stooans aint very big. You git these black uns

all roun this country. Thaiur's some good ole trees
at Bradnum, an some at Radnidge, but when th' ole
trees die they plant new kinds; but gi me th' ole
blacks—they taiak a lot a baitin."

c. "I suppoase ye sti-ull maiak th' ole baiacon-
badgur up heeur at Wheelur Eend?"

a. "Oh, ah; we do an pretty often; a good many
peepul maiak em."

c. "You know what they be then!"

a. "I should think e do! E often has one, an when
they be well done in a nice bit a su-ut dumplin it
maiaks a good dinnur fur any man as doos hard wurk.
Besides that, they be handy when ye be ettin them.
You can taiak it out a yu-ur baskut and hold it in yu-ur
hand; then ye can cut a paice auf wi yu-ur pockut-
knife, an lay it down anywheeur—ye dooant want a
pleeat. That's the way to finish up yu-ur leeavins
when ye a had fat baiacon fur a few days and gits
nee-ur the eend an it—that's the finist way to git rid
an it by a maiakin it up into a baiacon-badger."

c. "Well, dooant ye have anythin else in it biside
fat baiacon?"

a. "Oh, ah! we a summut else; if we had ony fat
baiacon in it, that ood be too fat fur some peepul.
Fust we chop up the baiacon into littul paices, then
mix em up wi chopped inen, an any co-ald taiaturs
ye a got left. Then ye maiak a roly-poly puddun
an it, sometimes neeurly a foot long. A coo-urse ye
a got to a one a these big long sasspans to bile it in.
When it's done, ye taiak it out, put it an a dish, an
taiak the cloth auf an it; then ye put it an the teeable
ready fur dinnur—and I dooant ceear how fat they
be, they can be as fat as any fat doe; all the beh-hur;

127

that's how I like em. When ye cut it up fur dinnur, ye jest taiak a cut athurt the middul; that a coo-urse is the best an its bekas it a got moast mait; but that dooant mattur to some, they like the eends wheeur thaiur's moast dumplin as much as the middul wheeur ye find moast mait."

(Enter D.)

"Hullo, Walt, an how be ye a gittin an?"

D. "Pritty well. How be you?"

A. "All right up to the presunt."

D. "Aint it a pity the reean kaips auf? It ood do no eend a good if we could git a five ur six hours' stiddy reean."

A. "It ood; but we shull a to put up wi what's sent us; tis no good compleeanin."

D. "I be pleeased to meet ye."

C. "An I be pleeasd to meet you. I dooant think as ivver I a met ye befu-ur, an I a sin ye a good many times down at West Wycombe, when ye were gooin to wurk. Bisides, mi dad an yu-ur dad were alwis the grettest friends, an they be boath dead now. I wish I had a spoke to ye befu-ur."

D. "Well, you nivver spoke to me when I passed ye down at West Wycombe."

C. "Well, I dint know ye were ole Tom's son; if e did e should ony a bin too glad to have had a few wurds wi ye. I wish ye had a spoke to me, bekas I shall alwis rimember yur ole dad, fur whenivver I met him he alwis had a kind wurd an a cheery smi-ul fur me. Ah, we miss th' ole feeaces; we shull nivver git sech fine ole fellurs as they used to be yeurs agoo."

D. "We shant; we shull nivver a the likes an em agen."

C. "I heeurd ye went through Palestine in the war."

D. "I did; went neeurly all ovur it, an see all kinds a peepul an heeurd all kinds a languages under the feeace a the sun. One fellur said to me one day, 'How many languages do you speeak?' and I said, 'Three—English, Scotch, an Irish.' "

C. "Well, you know another one."

D. "What's that?"

C. "Th' ole Bucks language."

D. "Gaw! so e did; but I furgot all about that."

C. "They doant speeak su much a that up heeur at Wheelur Eend as they used to yeeurs agoo, do they?"

D. "They do a bit now; Bacon's Bottom's the pleeace fur that. You should heeur em say, 'Fath-ur, this sah wunt cut,' an 'I can't git all this heeur ood in th' oodhus.' It ood taiak a foreigner ten thousand yeeurs to git to the top an bottom an it. Howivver could they understand a wurd like 'Lauk-a-massy-o'? They ood nivver understand it. Lauk-a-massy-o! Was thaiur ivver secch a wurd! You doant heeur that 1ow-a-deeas ony occasionally bi the oldur peepul. One night I was havin a geeam a cards wi sum peepul who come from London. All at once nobody played an the geeam come to a stop; so I said, 'Whosen turn?' One a the players looked up at me an said, 'What?' so I said agen, 'Whosen turn?' 'Well,' he said, 'I nivver heeurd sich a wurd as that afu-ur.' 'Ah,' I said, 'that's what we say at Wheelur Eend, an we a got some funny wurds up heeur. I cant stop; I shull a to goo.' "

BUCKINGHAMSHIRE DIALECT

c. "Can't ye tell us the tai-ul about the ole gahnder?"

D. "Ah; when mi ole mothur sold it to one a them hogs as be alwiz out to do ivverybody in! Well, one Chris-mus time this heeur fellur comes to mi mothur and wants to buy a goose; so she taiaks him out to the flock and pointin to one a that yee-ur's gollins (goslings), says, "Tha's the best! a that!" But bein a cunnin kind a cock he thought mi ole mothur was decaivin him. He went up to the flock and begun to cheeas an ole gahnder as had tramped Whaler Eend Common fur nigh an thurty yee-ur. At last he caught it and killed it and took it home. I cant stop any longur. I must goo! I ull tell ye the whool performance another time.

"I be pleased to see ye! Good night."

c. "So be I you! Good night!"

CHILDREN'S ESSAYS

EXAMPLES are given of compositions by children at various places in dialect. Whilst they may be looked upon as too artificial to be evidence of current dialect, they are obviously too ingenuous not to be the children's own simple thoughts, and they are trying to render these thoughts in the written expressions which are familiar to them.

This is a Gawcott girl's áccount of a visit to "Pressun Feeust," by which is meant Preston Bissett Feast:

It was a glarious ar'ernoon eesterday, an mi frien and I thaht about gooin tu Pressun Feeust, 'cas laast yeeur it pooured a reean an thundered quite evvy. We staar'ed about ah paast six an got theeur at seven. We ad a walk up the village and soon us see the band a-comin an it soon staar'ed playin. We wen to see ur ould friens an were pleeased to see em. Jest down a little strit theeur were swingin-booats an coocoanut shies. We saa the schooul, the charch, an the chapul. Theeur were crowds a folks a-taaking away fur all they were wuth; they kep axin us whether we liked it. It was jest about the saiam as Gaa-cutt Feeust, o-anly the weather was differant. I saa all mi owan brothers an sisters injoyin th'selves. In the middul a Pressun is a very ould pub caalled the 'Ould Hat,' which has a sign showin a greeat ould black hat. Soon us felt a spat a reean an thaht it bettur to tarn to'rds hoom. As us got neeur the ood it poured down summat aful, so us had to stand under a trai fur a few minutes; bu' when us got hoom it'd stopped.

In a composition written by Standard VI at Gawcott, *not* in dialect, occurred the following: "Before thunder bullocks very often *gad*." [1]

The following essay by a Haddenham child exhibits the bad and lazy habit of slurring *t*'s:

It was Sah-ur-day ar'ernoon an it ceeam an a-raianing like cats an dogs. I wahned to goo out to a pleeace, bu mother said I ad to goo to the shop to git some buhher, ceeak, chaise, an tay. So I said, I a behher weeat till it stops raianing or else I shull git wet, ant I? Mum said, Ees. Aher a liʲl while it stopped so I starh-ed. Jest es e got out a the geeat our dog ceeam a-runnin ah-er me. I threw a stooan a it bu it woont goo in agen bu follured me all the way up the streeat. It wai-ated outside the shop an when I starhed runnin back he ceeam aher me as fas as is legs ood carry im. He reeached hooam long a-fuur I did an wai-ated fur me at the geeat.

The two following conversations were written by two girls:

Waddesdon, 1924:

A. "Well, how be ye a-gittin an, maiat?"

B. "Not very well. I've had sich a ratten cold all the wake; eent bin up to it leeatly."

[1] The word is properly a substantive, and the phrase, according to Wright, is "get, or take the gad," the reference being to the gadfly, *Œstrus bovis*.

A. "Ah! colds be all the feshion now, eent em, old boey?"

B. "They be; as I was a-tellin yuur wife eesterday, they be all the goo."

A. "Howivver we shull a to put up wi em. I be jest a-gooin to faid them hogs as I be a-fattenin; be ye a-comin along to have a spy at em?"

B. "Ees, but I shant a to stop long as I want to teeak Dolly into Aylesbury, she's a good ole trotter."

A. "Ah, my wife talks about gooing to town to git her a new cooat. What do ye think an em?"

B. "They be some gret hogs. I shall have to be off now. Good marnin, ole chap."

A. "Good marnin, muster."

C. "Hullo, ole man, and how be ye?"

D. "Quite well thanks, maiat; how be them beeast a yourn a gittin an?"

C. "I give em keeak ivvery marnin, for I be a-fattenin em up fur Christmas, and they be a-gooin an fine. Ony eesterday I says to mi wife: Them beeast ull maiak some good baif."

D. "Ees, they ull, ole boy, you'll a some good mait if they keep an as they be now. Eesterday I went to markut and bought foour ship—they be some beauties. Put yur jackut an and come and look at em."

C (later). "Ah, they be fine ship."

THE HAYMAKING SONG

This was sung by Mr. Charles Styles, of Downley,
during Christmas 1926 at West Wycombe. Having
sung it in the villages on the west of High Wycombe
for half a century, he was able to give it with a zest
which delighted all who heard him:

A country boy be I,
   A rastic bred and barn,
The burds do sing, an so do I
   Rise at the arly marn.
I nivver waiast mi time away,
   Fur I'm alwiz to be seen,
As sun as the cock begins to crow,
   Out in the feeulds su greean.

     (Chorus, repeated after each verse.)

Out in the greean feeulds, su happy an su gay,
Out in the greean feulds a-reeakin up the hay,
Out in the greean feeulds I'll pass mi time away,
An like a lark I'll whissul in the marnin.

When sun be hot and land be dry
   I git the seeam, tis cleeur;
Tis then I stap to teeak a drap
   A stunnin home-brewed beeur.
Wi a tidy snack a luncheon aye
   At plough-tail all seree-an,
Cold beeans an baiacon, that's mi whack
   Out in the feeulds su greean.

My Dolly she's the finist lass
   Fur twenty mile around,
My Dolly she has rosy cheeks
   Hur aiquail cant be found.

When harvist hooam comes round, mi boys,
  Aich lass looks like a queean,
Oh, Doll and I! Oh, dont we dance
  Out in the feeulds su greean!

Some say the jolly joys a town
  Be jest the propur sorts,
Give I the cheeas, the hurdle reeace,
  And other country sports.
Breeakin their rest wi sprays a night
  Strong men are reerely seen,
I like the opun country best
  Out in the feeulds su greean.

GLOSSARY

[The following abbreviations are used : M.E.=Middle English, O.E. = Old English, I. = Ivinghoe.]

To compile a list of words seems to be a very mechanical task, the work of a harmless drudge, but those who have attempted it know that it may require as great qualities of omission and restraint as are to be found in literature and the fine arts. To record all one hears without regard to the speaker would certainly not prove the general use of a word. There are one or two words (such as our first one, *agate* = "in use") which are of North-Country origin and can only be counted as strays in Bucks. Words of general dialectal use, or possibly slang words (e.g. *whapping* = "large"), have not been included; similarly it was felt unnecessary to bring in words like *skimpy* or *trapes*, which have earned a place in such a familiar standard work as the *Concise Oxford Dictionary*. The spelling of Dr. Wright's great *Dialect Dictionary* has been adopted; a closer approximation to the local sound is given where it differs from this. The very common verb *to ox about* = "to become covered with mud," represents the invariable pronunciation of a word which has often to be used in the Vale in winter. It is to be found in Wright's work as "hockse."

Besides words furnished by Mr. Harman, the chief sources of supply have been the lists printed by Mr. A. H. Cocks in the seventh and ninth volumes of the *Records of Bucks*; the long list contained in the last-named volume owes most of its worth to the research of Mr. F. G. Gurney, and such words are

generally to be found below with the addition of
" I.," for Ivinghoe, to them. The present editor
added some collected by himself; some of them have
been printed before.

Three phrases from Ivinghoe have been omitted
from the list as possibly representing the exercise of
particular imagination in that place rather than
general dialectal use. They are too good, however,
to be omitted from this record. One is the applica-
tion of the phrase "sheep's-head-and-pluck" to
describe the Dutch wall clock with long pendulum;
here the metaphor is drawn from the dressed carcase
of a sheep, where the trachea and lungs are left
dependent from the head. Another is the use of the
name "Benny Gaunt," jocularly applied to the sun;
the phrase is illustrated by a heavy sheaf of corn
which the labourer who lifted it called "one of Benny
Gaunt's dumplin'-busters." This Mr. Gurney rightly
calls "a triumph of metaphor," and adds the note that
Ben Gaunt or Caunt was a famous prize-fighter in
the neighbourhood. The third Ivinghoe phrase explains a "nice derangement" of metaphors rather than
a dialectal use. An old man "as weren't 'alf sharp"
received a blow on the head from a stone thrown by
a boy: "You 'nation young rogue," he cried, "you've
bin and rose a dent on me 'ead as big as a walnut's
egg." The beauty of this grows upon one as one
ponders over it.

The greater number of what Professor Wyld calls
"regional dialect" words, after all, are "genuine cor-
ruptions of words which the yokel has heard from
educated speakers, or read, misheard, or misread, and
ignorantly altered and adopted, often with a slightly

twisted significance. Probably many hundreds of 'dialect' words are of this origin, and have no historical value whatever, except inasmuch as they illustrate a general principle in the modification of speech." [1]

On the other hand, words will be found in the subjoined list which are not Received Standard English, and have yet been derived from Old English words which have not been generally accepted in this particular form. Examples of this are to be found in "wanty," the belly-band of harness which keeps the chain traces in position, and "stale," the shaft or handle of a tool. Both these words are very generally used, as is shown by their occurrence in printed sale-catalogues.

Generally speaking, all the words given have been heard at places far removed from each other in the county; changing practice and customs, standard education, and, above all, the facilities of modern locomotion are doing away with their use so rapidly that it is more difficult every year to collect them or even to confirm their meanings. In the course of another generation the list will certainly be much diminished.

AGATE.—In use. "We got fower beds agate in our 'ouse." (I.) A word of Northern use, and possibly a stray in Bucks.

ANEWST, NEAWEST, NEAWIST.—Used only in the expression "anewst the matter" with the meanin "pertaining to." Wright cites O.E. *neah-wist*, nearness, neighbourhood.

---

[1] *A History of Modern Colloquial English,* p. 14.

AWEVER.—This has not the meaning of "however,"
but is an emphatic expletive at the end of a sen-
tence, with the meaning "at any rate." Examples
are: "I see'd 'im goo, I see'd 'im at the geate
awever"; "E might a-gin me a pint awever."

AX.—Ask. O.E. *acsian*, to ask.

BAGGING IN THE HAULM.—Cutting the high stubble
when corn was reaped with a sickle. The phrase
necessarily died with the process, but the smooth-
edged hook used for cutting small pieces of corn
is still called a "bagging-hook," more often a
"fagging hook," *q.v.*

BAG-SOPS.—When a field of corn was fagged, the
labourer used to take the bottom of a loaf of
bread, cut it in two, and place a piece of lard
between the two pieces. When he had his
dinner, he took the crumb of the bread, placed
it in a basin of small-beer, and ate it as sop.
This was the "bag-sop"; the crust he ate with
the lard. (Wright gives "bagging" as "food
taken in the forenoon"—always as a North-
Country word.)

BAMMOCK.—To strike, as when driving in a stake.

BANSTICKLE.—The stickleback (*Gasterosteus tra-
churus*). (I.)

BARYARD.—Two sticks joining a third and larger
piece of timber at an acute angle, placed at the
back of a two-wheeled cart to keep it horizontal.

BAT-FOWLING.—Catching birds at night from the
eaves of houses by means of a net attached to
poles, i.e. "bats."

BATTER.—A sloping bank. Very common; said of
a rabbit which had been shot: "E come tiddly-

bump down the batter." As used by builders for a wall with a slope receding from the bottom, it is a dictionary word.

BEAR.—If a cart is so loaded that the weight presses on the horse's back, it is said to "bear." Conversely, when the load is so far back that the shafts are raised, it is said to "hang."

BEE-NETTLE.—White dead-nettle (*Lamium album*). (I.)

BELLUS (*for* BELLIS).—To bustle about. Said to one who loaded coal expeditiously: "Wha be at? Clawin an bellusin about? Ant yu got pert nigh a ton an? Yu maant put a lot more an." Aylesbury, September 1928.

BENNET.—Long, coarse grass. O.E. *beonet*.

BESOM.—A woman of a loose character. (I.)

BEVER *or* BAIVER.—Drink taken between meals, usually in forenoon. O.E. *beivre*, a drinking.

BIBLE-BACKED.—Used of a cow with a somewhat convex back. (Wright quotes it as used of persons only.)

BISNINGS *or* BISSEN (*a variant of* BEESTINGS).—The thick, rich milk given by a newly calved cow, colostrum. O.E. *bystyng*.

BLATE.—To bellow. A common proverb is, "A blatin cow soon forgets her calf," referring to the noise made by the mother for twenty-four hours after the removal of her calf, and applied, as a metaphor, to exaggerated grief.

BLIND-EYES.—The scarlet poppy (*Papaver rheas*). (I.) There is a superstition that if this flower is looked at for too long a time, the gazer will lose his sight.

BLIZZY.—A blazing fire.

BODGEL.—To bundle up in a careless fashion. This was applied to workers in the chair-factories who assembled the parts of a chair.

BOOARD (*for* BODE).—Foretell. "I booard wet." (Downley.) O.E. *bodian*, to announce.

BOSS, BOSSY, BONSOR, BAWNSOR.—A large ball of stone or glass used in marble-playing. The marbles are placed in a ring and the boss is rolled at them so as to displace as many as possible. (Dinton, West Wycombe, etc.)

BOUGH-HOUSE.—A booth with a temporary licence to sell beer. Within living memory seen at Ivinghoe Fair, an interesting survival of the mediæval custom which led to the proverb. (See also allusion to this on p. 64.)

BOUT.—In ploughing, the length of a furrow and back again.

BRANSING.—Presumably "brands' ends," the pieces of wood which drop from the fire-dogs when a log burns through in the middle. This particular form is not given by Wright, but is common in the Chilterns.

BREVIT *or* BRIVIT.—To fidget. *Records of Bucks* (VII, 288) gives the meaning as "to rummage," quoting its use at Winslow.

BRITCH (*for* BREECH).—To place money in the pocket. "I britched him with a shilling." (Downley.) Wright's use in this sense is confined to the passive: "to be breeched," to be rich.

BROWSING.—A cow's manger.

BRY (*variant of* BREEZE).—The gadfly. O.E. *briosa.*

BULL-RATTLE.—White campion (*Lychnis alba*). (I.)

BULLRUSH, BULLROOSH.—To go headlong (Chesham).

BURROW.—Shelter, shade. A Gawcott thatcher, when asked if he had been in the wind, replied, "No; I a bin in the burruh all the time."

BURY (*or* BERRY) OF WITCHERT.—One layer of wichert forming the wall of a house, etc. (See Appendix.)

CAGGLE.—To argue or dispute. (Dinton.) Not in Wright. Query whether a mere corruption of "haggle."

CAGMAG.—Disorder, tangle. (I.) "All in a cagmag," said of hair, yarn, etc. Wright does not give this meaning, his fifth use of the first substantive means "a fix, a hobble."

CARR.—To carry. An old man who generally acted as bearer at funerals said, "If there's as many to carr me as I've a-carr'd, the chu'chyard'll be proper full." (Weston Turville.)

CHAIR BODGER.—Man who turns chair-legs with a pole-lathe in the woods. The usual meaning of "bodger" as a clumsy worker by no means applies, nor is it allied with "bodgel," *q.v.* Query whether a variant of "badger," a licensed dealer, originally in corn, but applied to all trades.

CHAM.—To chew, bite. (West Wycombe.)

CHAMPER.—An instrument for cutting off the "ail," or beard, of barley. (Sale catalogue at Prestwood, 1903.) *Vide sub* HUMMELER.

CHIBBLE.—To gnaw, as a mouse does. (Wing, Gawcott, etc.)

CHUCK-THONG.—The strap to a headstall, under the chin. Wright's sixth meaning of "chuck" is "the throat," but he does not give the compound word.

CLA.—To seize (claw), to move hastily. "Cla holt" = grasp quickly. "The whistle blew, and lor! I cla-a-hed in." (I.)

CLANGER.—A bacon clanger is the same at Gawcott as the "bacon badger" of the Vale, i.e. a dumpling. Apparently allied with "clung," of which Wright's sixth meaning is "close, heavy, sad."

CLAPERED.—Splashed with mud, bedraggled. "He come in claypered up to his neck-'ole." (Slapton, Wing.)

CLAPSE or CLOPS.—Two vertical pieces of wood, of which one is hinged at the base and can be shut behind the horns of a cow when being milked. The cow can move her head vertically, but cannot interfere with her neighbours or turn her head round.

CLATS.—The dung of cattle. Wright compares Danish *klat*, which means a " clod of earth, dirt."

CLOB-HEAD (*for* CLUB-HEAD).—The miller's thumb (*Cottus gobio*); also a blockhead. The dual meaning is illustrated by a story from Ivinghoe, which embodies the answer of an old man who was gathering brook-lime. "Sin any fish?" asked a passer-by. "No, I aint," he replied sourly, "there aint ne'er a one; but there's a d——d gurt clobhead not fur awff."

COCKAMUMPRIN.—Posturing. (I.) Not given by Wright, though his second use of the verb "cock" means "to swagger, strut, show off."

CODGEL *or* COTCHEL.—To contrive, economise. "His grammer codgelled up an ole pat-ball for 'im." (I.)

COFER.—A large chest. Cocks (*Records,* IX, 134) spells this "cofa," and will not allow it to be a corruption of "coffer." In this Wright appears to differ entirely from him; the word is sounded as though spelt with one *f.*

COLT (*for* CALL).—Occasion; necessity. "You've no colt to do it" = you need not. (Ford, Dinton.)

CONSARN (*variant of* CONCERN).—"Used imprecatively" is Wright's ninth explanation of the word. "Consarn the thing!" (Ford, Dinton.)

COTCHEL.—A sack of corn partly filled. (Wheeler End and West Wycombe.)

COUNTRY.—One's own district or area, apart from others. At Stokenchurch some years ago, and at Aston Abbotts still (1928), residents spoke of their villages as "our country."

COVENTREE.—The mealy guelder-rose (*Viburnum lantana*). (Hambleden.) The young wood of this tree is pliable and practically unbreakable.

CREEPING-JINNY.—Moneywort (*Lysimachia nummularia*).

CRIBBLING.—Lame. "E gooes proper cribblin." (I.) This is Wright's third meaning: "a cripple."

CUFF.—The glove, made of whit-leather, used by a hedger. Not given by Wright.

CUNNING.—Wise, able, shrewd, knowing. "I'm sure that child won't live; it's too cunning." (Quainton, 1924.) In the south of the county an entertainment was held, but at the end of the performance the money paid for entrance was missing. The next day the committee decided to employ a "cunning man" to unravel the mystery; he came before them and was asked by the janitor of the entertainment whether he could find the thief. "Yes," was the answer; "if you go upstairs and peep in the looking-glass, you'll see un."

DAME.—The mistress of the house, especially the wife of a yeoman. Fairly common in the South until 1890.

DANDY-GO-RUSSET.—Said of a faded or rusty-coloured garment. (I.) This seems to be a stray word from the west; Wright quotes it from Devon and Cornwall.

DIBBY.—Intoxicated.

DIDDICOY.—A gipsy (I. and Gawcott.) Wright gives "diddiky," meaning "a gipsy's kettle."

DIDGE (*variant of* DODGE).—To make the best of bad circumstances. "We ull didge along as well as we can." (Gawcott and Dinton.)

DILLING.—The smallest and weakest of a litter.

DINGLE.—To dawdle. "When we do have a practice, we can nivver git on when we begin; after we've gone on a little time, the others come a-dinglin in one by one." (Drayton Parslow.)

DINK, DINKS.—(1) To toss, dandle a baby. (Waddesdon.) (2) To walk in an affected manner. (I.) Used as we sometimes say "dance off" in the following phrase from Gawcott: "Then I had to goo a-dinksing down to the doctur fur a certificate."

DISANNUL.—To inconvenience, to disarrange, to put about. (North Marston.)

DITHER.—A tremble, shake, or shiver. "I be all of a dither." (Drayton Parslow.) "He's got the ditherums." (Wheeler End.)

DOCITY.—Spirit, animation. "This mungy weather mommers me; it makes me feel summat unkid, as if I'd no docity in me." (Newport Pagnell.)

DRAWTER *or* DRATER.—A piece of cloth drawn over the lace on a pillow when the pins have been removed, in order to keep it clean.

DROTCHEL.—A sloven, a slut. (I.) Wright gives it as a variant of "dratchel," but quotes "drotchel" from Johnson as "an idle wench, a sluggard."

DRUCKSY (*variant of* DROXY).—Unsound, rotten. Wright says it is derived from *drix*, the decayed part of timber.

DRUG-BAT.—A drag or shoe placed under a wheel to prevent it from turning round. *Records of Bucks* (VII, 291), gives "drogue," a timber cart. (Marlow.) The phrase "drug-bat" occurs on a notice-board on the hill to the north of Medmenham.

DUFF-END.—The shortened thatch at the end of a rick. (Simpson, Gawcott.) Not given by Wright, who has "duffie," blunt, round-headed, from the Orkney Islands.

DUMMEL.—(1) Dull-edged (of a tool). (2) Dull-witted (of a man). (3) Damp or limp (of cut corn). (Hambleden.) Wright gives many illustrations, but all with meaning (2), i.e. personal.

ECCLE (*for* HICKWALL).—Green woodpecker (*Gecinus viridis*). Wright gives thirty-three variants of "hickwall," for which words he cites various authors from 1580. He quotes "heckle" as used in Bucks from *Nature Notes*, No. 10.

ECHE (*variant of* EKE).—(1) Verb, to make go as far as possible. (2) Subst., ring of plaited straw added to beehive. (Chesham.)

EGGLER.—An itinerant merchant who buys eggs for re-sale. The word is "Iggler" for "Higgler," now popularly associated with traffic in eggs.

ELDERN.—The elder-tree. O.E. *ellaern*.

ETCHELS.—Used in the phrase "thick as etchels," and applied, e.g., to a crop of mangolds. If the word be the same as "hatchels," it is used in Northants, according to Wright, with the meaning of "a small row or cock of cut grass."

FAGGING HOOK.—A reaping hook. Apparently the first meaning is that of a crooked stick with which corn or grass is drawn to one side for cutting. The fagging (or bagging) hook has a smooth edge which has to be constantly whetted with a stone, distinguishing it thus from the sickle, the curve of which was also different.

FALL IN THE WAY WITH, FALL IN HER ARMS.—To be pregnant. Wright has many phrases similar to the above with a kindred meaning, but none exactly the same. "She'll soon have something fall in her arms" is the usual gossip's saying in Bucks.

FEASE.—To hurry away. "Cam an, let's be feasin." (Downley, near Wycombe.)

FELT, FALT.—The fieldfare (*Turdus pilaris*). (West Wycombe.)

FERRUCKING.—Poking about. Said of animals scratching at door of hutch. (Marlow.) Wright gives "ferrick," to fidget, to move about restlessly.

FETT.—Preterite tense of "fetch." O.E. *fetian*, pret. *fetode*. (Woughton, Gawcott, Bledlow Ridge.)

FIERCE.—Lively, vigorous, in good spirits. A healthy child is "fierce and hale."

FILLYLOO.—An uproar.

FLAXEN, FLAXING.—A comb. Sometimes "flacking comb." Wright gives "flax" as the fur of an animal, and "fleck" is used in this way of the hair of rabbits and hares at Marlow. (*Records of Bucks*, VII, 292).

FLIGGED.—Full-fledged, able to fly. (I.)

FLIPPUT.—"Potato flipput" is potato sop. (Wheeler End.) Query whether cognate with "flip," any weak, insipid liquor, given by Wright from Northants.

FLIT.—To tie by a rope, to tether. (I.) Wright gives its meaning as "to shift a tethered animal from one spot to another." An interesting use of the word occurs in the Cartulary of Missenden Abbey (Sloane MS. 747, f. 66), "Whan the stede ys stole than flytte the stable dore."

FLUMMOX, FLUMMOCKS.—To bewilder, puzzle, confound.

FORM.—To imagine, conceive. (I.)

FORREST.—Foremost.

FRAMMARD *and* TOE'ARD.—In ploughing, the earth is

thrown "fromward," or from the land, and "toward," or on to the land, when the plough returns in the opposite direction.

FRET.—To thaw. (I.)

FRIM.—Soft, tender, succulent. Wright quotes O.E. *frym*, vigorous.

FRORN.—Frozen. Wright's thirteenth form of the past participle.

FUNCH.—To push or thrust. In playing the game at marbles called "ring-taw," the ally had to be propelled as far from the ring as possible by the thumb only; if the hand were jerked as well, the distance was nearly doubled. This push was the true "funch," but, being contrary to the true game, the word came to be synonymous with "cheat" or "shuffler." (West Wycombe.)

GALLUS.—Very, exceedingly. This intensive use of the word as an adverb is Wright's eleventh meaning. Earlier meanings have a rascally, mischievous, or impudent connotation; the shadow of the *gallows* rests on them.

GAMBREL.—A crooked piece of wood used to hang up carcases with.

GARM (*variant of* GAUM).—To daub, soil, make dirty.

GEELY-BALK.—The iron bar fixed across the chimney from which the pot-hooks and chains hung. (North Bucks.) *Records of Bucks* (IX, 142) says that it is often used for the pot-hooks and chains themselves.

GLIBBY.—Slippery.

GLIME.—To glance sideways, amorously, or distrustfully. (I.)

GOGGY (? *variant of* GOBBITY).—Soft, tender, toothsome; as applied to fat—the opposite of "reasy," *q.v.* (I.)

GOOLY-BEE, GOOLY-BUG.—For "goldy-bug," the ladybird (*Coccinella septempunctata*). (Ivinghoe and Wing.)

GRANDMOTHER'S NEEDLE.—Valerian. (Chesham.) Not given by Wright.

GRUMPIN, GRUMPLIN.—The horizontal timber just above ground-level used in the construction of a timber-framed house. A corruption of "ground-pin." Also called "grunsill" (i.e. ground-sill).

GRUNTY.—Tough, in phrase "grunty ash." Almost certainly a corruption of "ground-ash."

GUDGELL.—Mud, drainage. "That there ditch's brimful o' filthy gudgel." (I.)

HACK AND HAMMER ABOUT.—To hum and haw, to hesitate; Wright's 27th meaning.

HACKLE (*invariably* ACKLE).—To dress, to get oneself ready. Wright cites O.E. *hacele*, a cloak. The word is the same as that applied to the crest of the neck feathers of the domestic cock and to the priest's vestment.

HAG-HAW *or* AGAR.—The haw, the fruit of the hawthorn-tree. O.E. *haga*, the fruit of the hawthorn. At Ivinghoe "hahs-bush" is used for the hawthorn.

HAGGLE-CART.—A horse and cart let out on hire to do rough work or odd jobs. (Winslow and Ivinghoe.) Wright quotes the term from the *Oxford Times* of 7th January, 1899. The proprietor and driver is commonly called the "haggle-cart man," and his personal name is ignored.

HAGGLED (*always* AGGLED).—Wearied, harassed, worn out.

HAINED.—Of grass: preserved for hay, not used for mowing. (Winslow.)

HARLICKING (ARLICKING).—Acting in a foolish manner. Not given by Wright, who quotes "harlican" from *Jude the Obscure* as a "term of abuse." There seems to be no other source of derivation than "harlequin."

HARR (AR).—The heel-post of a gate, to which the hinge is fastened.

HARRUP.—(1) To dig or "muss" (of dogs). (2) To nag. (I.) See *Records of Bucks* (IX, 144), where Mr. Gurney will not allow meaning (2) to be connected with "harp," but supposes it from the same root as "harrow."

HATCHEL.—A small row of cut grass, raked up after tedding. (Gawcott and Steeple Claydon.)

HAY-BEECH, HORNED-BEECH.—The horn-beam.

HAY-BIRD.—(1) The whitethroat (*Sylvia cinerea*). (2) Blackcap (*Sylvia atricapilla*). Wright gives (2), but says that the word is applied to any bird building its nest of hay, as does the whitethroat.

HAZLE (*verb and subst.*), HAZEL (*adj.*).—To dry on the surface in the sun.

HEATHER (*variant of* EDDER).—To bind the top of a newly laid hedge with hazel, bramble, or other pliable rod. Wright quotes O.E. *eodor*, enclosure, fence.

HEDGE - POKER.—The hedge - sparrow (*Accentor modularis*). (West Wycombe.)

HIND-ER (*for* HIND-CLOTH).—The cloth which covers the entire lace-pillow when it is not in use.[1]

HOBHOUCHIN (OBOWCHIN).—Apparently applied to various insects—a large heavy moth at Ivinghoe, and a cockchafer at Wendover. (*Records of Bucks*, IX, 154.) Wright quotes a note in Ellis's *Modern Husbandry*, 1750, to the effect that it is applied in Bucks to the Peacock and Red Admiral butterflies, but not to white ones.

HOCKSY (*invariably* OXY).—Muddy, soft, sticky. Also used as a verb. "To go ocksing about" is to move in a slovenly way.

HODMANDOD.—A snail. Sometimes called "hoddydod."

HOMMOCK.—A large, awkward foot or leg. This is Wright's third meaning; his seventh is the verbal use "to walk with a clumsy, awkward gait"; this is also used in *Bucks Records* (VII, 294).

HOTCHEL.—To hobble, limp. (Winslow, Padbury.)

HUCKET (*for* HICKET).—To sob, to gasp for breath. "Stop hucketting this mominit." (I.)

HUGGLE *or* HUCKLE.—To stoop, crouch. "I sat ere uckled up chimley." (I.) The substantive (meaning "the hip") is not in general use in Bucks.

HUMMELER.—An instrument to remove the awns of barley (see also *sub* CHAMPER). The original

---

[1] Given by T. Wright, *The Romance of the Lace Pillow*, p. 119, but not by J. Wright, *Dialect Dictionary*.

meaning is "hornless," cf. Low German *hummel*, a hornless beast.

IDLE-FRIG, -FREG, -FRECK, *or* -FEG.—A hang-nail, or broken skin by the quick of the finger-nail. (Chesham, Ivinghoe, Wing.)

JIPPER.—The broth in which a rabbit, etc. is cooked.

JIRRUP.—An underhand throw. (West Wycombe.) Presumably a corruption of "jerk."

KEACH.—To dip for water. *Records of Bucks* (VII, 294) quotes a local paper which refers to the filthy condition of ponds in the Naphill district in 1893: "all public keech ponds." Used of emptying a sump or cess-pool at Wendover. The spelling, with this meaning, should be "ke*a*ch," according to Wright. Used at Quainton, in 1926, of the ponds on the green.

KIBBLE.—To walk lame, especially of a horse. (I.)

KID.—The pod, or seed-vessel, of peas, beans, etc. "I set two rows athirt the garden, an they kidded beautiful." (Weston Turville.)

KISS-I'-MY-CORNER.—Lad's love, or southern-wood (*Artemisia abrotanum*). (I.) Wright has "kiss-me-quick-and-go," from Devonshire.

KIVER.—A shallow vessel of wood, oval in shape, used in making butter, etc. Used in auctioneer's catalogue, 1922. Wright suggests association with French *cuvier*, a bathing-tub. A sale catalogue at Stoke Hammond, 1881, includes a "dough kiver." The O.E.D. cites *cyf*, a tub.

KRETCH (*for* CRATCH), in phrase "pig kretch."—A frame, shaped like a broad ladder, supported on legs, and curved downwards, upon which pigs are laid to be killed.

KURLICK.—Charlock (*Sinapis arvensis*). Invariably so called.

LADDIKIN.—A bone instrument for opening window lead, to fit in the glass. (I.)

LAIN.—A layer. "The next lain'll begin drawing in for the ruff." (Hambleden.)

LATTERMATH.—The second crop of grass which grows after a field has been mown. From *latter* and O.E. *maeth*, a mowing.

LATTERN.—Late. Used of cherries, etc., to denote a crop which ripens last, in contrast with the early or "forrard" varieties.

LEAR.—Empty, faint with hunger. Wright cites M.E. *lere*, empty, and O.E. *lœre*.

LEASE.—To glean. O.E. *lesan*, to gather.

LINGE.—Consistency; used, e.g., in describing the mixing of a suet pudding, when the due absorption of water, flour, and suet is reached. (Askett, see p. 42 and West Wycombe.) Wright gives Hampshire adjective with the meaning "pliable."

LINGE.—To loosen. (Chesham.) Apparently not given by Wright, unless it be connected with verb "linch," to beat severely, which he associates with the Norman dialect word "lincher," "*donner un coup de fouet.*"

LITCHUP.—An idle person, a loafer. Also used as verb. (I.) See *Records of Bucks* (IX, 150), where root suggested is M.E. *lich*, a corpse. Not given by Wright.

LOGGER.—A straw-plaiting term to denote seven splints of straw. (I.)

LOPPETING.—Slouching, shambling, loitering.

MAMMER *or* MUMMER.—To confuse, perplex. The first form used at Haddenham, the second at Aston Abbotts.

MAWKIN.—The mop used for cleaning the hot embers from a brick-oven before the bread is put in. This is Wright's fourth meaning; the word is a diminutive of the name Maud, and is used successively for a girl, a slut, a scarecrow, and a mop.

MAWKS (*for* MAWKIN).—*See above.* "You great mawks." (Downley.) Here it was used rather as a "tomboy."

MILKY.—Half-heartedly, timidly. (I.) Not given by Wright; he gives "milk-hearted," as meaning "poor-spirited," however.

MOLLY-PEART (*for* MALAPERT).—Saucy. "That there colt's a good deal better neow, that it be; awever, that's gittin quoite mollypeart." (Wing.)

MOP-YAWNEY.—A stupid. (West Wycombe.) A combination of "mope," to go about in an aimless fashion, and "yawney," a fool.

MOT *or* PITCHMOT.—A game in which a small stone or button was pitched at a mark. Played with ha'pence it became a gambling game, and he whose ha'penny fell nearest the mark took all the others, tossed them up, and kept those which fell "heads." (West Wycombe.)

MOWSTEAD (*pronounced* MOUSE-TED).—The vertical partition against the threshing-floor in a barn which prevents the corn from falling back into the bays. (Wherever a mowstead has been left *in situ*, it is known by that name all over the county. Strangely enough, it is not amongst the various meanings given by Wright, though all are associated with barns or ricks of corn.)

MOZE (*for* MOSE).—To smoulder, to burn slowly without flame. (Winslow.) The word at Chesham is "moult" (*Records of Bucks*, IX, 152).

MUGGERUM, MUGGERALS (*properly* MIDGERUM).—The leafy fat belonging to the intestine of an animal, especially a pig.

MULLEN.—A headstall, or leather halter for a horse.

MULLOCK.—Dirt, rubbish. Land which has become foul with weeds is said to be full of mullock. "Never mind the mullock, 't ull kaip the damp in the ground." (Gawcott.) (Also Drayton Parslow, Westbury; general in the N.W.)

MUNGY (of weather).—Warm, damp.

NAIF.—To steal. (West Wycombe.) Probably connected with "neive." Wright does not give this precise meaning, which must be "to take a handful of anything."

NATCHY (*for* GNATTERED).—Ill-tempered, peevish, irritable. (Downley.) The use of this word is given by Wright chiefly in the northern counties, though Warwickshire is cited.

NIFF-NAFFS.—Trifles. (West Wycombe.)

NIGH-HAND.—Nearly. "It's nigh-hand to four o'clock." (I.)

NUNCHEON.—Luncheon. "Master, tis nuncheon time; I be gooin to a my nuncheon." (Gawcott.) Wright gives it as in general dialectal use, and derives it from M.E. *noneschenche,* a donation for drink to workmen.

NUTHER (*for* NEITHER).—"E's nuther ard ood nur bush-faggot" (I.), meaning "neither good nor bad."

OAT-FLYERS.—The husks or chaff of oats.

OVER-RIGHT.—Opposite. (Very general.)

PADWAY.—The central part of a cart-track between the ruts. (I. and Hambleden.)

PEN-THRUSH.—The missel-thrush. (Gawcott.)

PICKID *or* PICKET.—Peaked, pointed. "You know as it's barley by they pickut eends." (Stoke Mandeville.)

PIMMOCK.—Dainty and fanciful as to food. The adjective "pimmocky" is very commonly used.

PITCHING.—A stone or brick-paved path or yard.

POODLE (*variant of* PUDDLE).—To hobble; to walk about slowly and feebly. "He came poodlin arter us." (I.)

PURRUL (*variant of* PURL).—Applied to a form of straw-plait made with four unsplit straws.

QUIFF.—A hint. (West Wycombe.)

QUILT.—To swallow. (West Wycombe.)

QUILTER.—Anything very large, a "whopper." When the ponds at Stowe were cleaned out, they were full of fish, "and they were some quilters too." (Gawcott.)

RACKWAY.—Path cut through wood. (Gawcott.) Wright gives this meaning all over England, and quotes Dutch *rak,* a track.

RAG.—The lower chalk, dug from a rag-pit. Commonly used everywhere along the Chiltern escarpment. Wright gives the word for various kinds of stone, but not for chalk.

RANNY.—A shrew (*Sorex araneus*) ; the short-tailed fieldmouse (*Mus agrestis*).

REASY (*for* REASTY).—Rancid; especially used of bacon which has become yellow and strong-tasting.

RIDDY-POLE.—The bar across a wide chimney to which the pot-hangers were attached. (Simpson.) Afterwards applied (by a kind of synecdoche) to the hanger itself. (Bletchley.)

RIDGET.—The chain which passes over the saddle on a horse's back and supports the shafts. The converse piece of harness is the wantey, *q.v.*

RODNEY.—One who hangs about to do odd jobs, such as holding horses, opening locks on canals, etc. (I.) This is Wright's third use of the word.

ROWK (*for* RAUK).—To stir about, rake.

ROOKER, RUCKER.—Said of a horse that will not draw steadily. "He's a reglar rooker." (Ford, Dinton.) Apparently not given by Wright, though his sixth use of the verb "to ruck" is "to strain, jerk, twist."

ROWSTING.—Buffeting. Query a corruption of "roistering."

RUCKET (*pronounced* RUCKUT).—Lumber, rubbish. Used at a sale: "That's a lot of ruckut." (Ford, Dinton.)

SCRARM.—(?) *variant of* SCRAMB, which Wright gives as meaning "to rake together with the hands; to scratch; to pull down violently."

SCROBBLE.—Broken sticks and odd pieces. (Dinton.)

Wright has *scrabble* with the meaning "stunted tree; thorns and briers."

SCROBBLE.—To scramble.

SCURF (*variant of* SCUFF).—Given as "to punish" at Chesham. (*Records of Bucks*, IX, 160.) Wright's third use is "to strike, to cuff."

SEEDLIP, SEDLIP, SIDLIP.—A basket used to hold the seed when broadcasting. (Catalogue of 1879.) Also called "sidcut," for "seedcote."

SHACKLES.—Vegetable soup.

SHAMBLES.—The fore ladder, or framework attached to a cart for carrying hay, etc. The corresponding one at the back is called the "in-ladder." (Auctioneer's catalogues.)

(1) SHIRT-BUTTONS, (2) SOLDIER'S-BUTTONS.—The greater stitchwort (*Stellarea holostea*). (1) Beaconsfield. (2) Chesham. Wright gives No. 1 in various counties, but he cites No. 2 as herb Robert in S. Bucks, and elsewhere as goosegrass, burdock, marsh marigold (which seems most appropriate), and burnet rose.

SHIVE ABOUT.—To wander aimlessly.

SHIVER.—A slice, especially of bread. Wright compares it with Icelandic *skifa*, a slice.

SHORE, SHORRY.—A stick for carrying hurdles or a faggot.

SHUT IN *or* OUT.—To put a horse in (or take out of) the shafts. Commonly used over most of the county.

SKEG.—The bullace (*Prunus insititia*).

SLEER.—To move away in a sneaking fashion.

SLOMMUCK (*for* SLAMMOCK).—An untidy person,

a sloven. It is said that "sotchel" is used with a similar meaning; not given by Wright.

SLOTCHKIN.—Slovenly, untidy. Wright compares Icelandic *sloka,* to slop.

SMALM.—(1) To smear, to daub. "Splahm" is used at Gawcott and at Wheeler End, with the same meaning; not given by Wright. The same word is perhaps to be found in this instruction for spreading manure: "It's no good puttin on that dabbitin little bit; you wants to smawsum round em." (Dinton.) (2) A further use of the word "smalm" is "to curry favour by obsequiousness." Is this cognate with the use given in (1) in the same way as the verb "butter" is colloquially used of excessive flattery?

SMELL-SMOCK.—The flower usually (and more elegantly) called ladysmock (*Cardamine pratensis*).

SNOTBERRIES, SNOTTERGOBS.—Yew berries. (Slapton and I.)

SOLLOP.—Meadow-sorrel. (South of the county.) See also SOUR-GOGS.

SOODLE, SUDDLE.—To dawdle, to saunter. (I.) Occurs frequently in Clare's poems.

SOUR-GOGS.—Corruption of "sour-sogs," or meadow-sorrel (*Rumex acetosa.*) (Woughton.) See also SOLLOP.

SPICKET *and* FOSSETT.—This is a phonetic rendering of "spigot and faucet," which occurs in the catalogue of a sale at Quainton in 1876 in the following words: "Lot 98. Two brewing tubs, tun bowl, spicket and fossett."

SPRAWT (*for* SPROT).—Small twigs or sticks. "I be

jest a-gooin to pick up they sprawts." (Waddesdon.)

SPREEZY.—Splitting or warping of timber. (Hambleden.) Not given by Wright, who has
"spreak," to sprain.

STALE.—The handle, shaft, or stave of an implement
or tool. The general term; an invoice from a
wheelwright at Weston Turville dated 1928
reads: "One stale for a beetle." O.E. *stœla*, a
stalk.

STEM.—The main body of a rick, neither top nor
bottom.

STIVE.—To keep close and warm; to suffocate, stifle.
"He were stived up in a little ol ole so
as he couldn't hardly move." (I., West
Wycombe.)

STOACH.—To come slowly. (*Records of Bucks*, IX,
165, citing Chesham, but query this?). Wright
gives it as "to trample in mud or water; to tread
wet ground in holes."

STOCK-AXE.—A kind of pick-axe used for grubbing
up trees, the two pointless ends being flattened
in the same plane as the handle, and at right
angles with it, respectively.

STOOP *or* STEEP.—To tilt a barrel to make the con-
tents flow more freely. When so tilted, it is
supported with a "scotch," or wedge.

STORCHING ABOUT.—Behaving in a vain manner.
(Wheeler End.) Corruption of stalking?

STULCH.—Layers of straw as placed by the thatcher.
The art of good thatching lies in keeping the
stulches even.

SWADE.—Grass-land, old pasture. Wright says it is the same word as "swath."

TAN.—Then. (An expression "now and tan" used at Wheeler End.)

'TANDRA *or* 'TANDRA-WIG.—A cake eaten on St. Andrew's Day, 11th December. (I.)

TANKET.—To follow persistently. "What do ye want then, tanketin arter me all the whoild?" (I.) Query whether this is more than a corruption of "dangling."

TANTADLIN.—A small, light tart. (I.) Very wide dialectal use, according to Wright.

TEELER.—The peg which holds the noose of a rabbit-snare in position. Wright's fourth use of the word is "the part of a trap or gin to which the bait is attached." The verb "to teel" means "to place anything so that it may fall, to set a trap."

TEEN (*variant of* TEND).—To kindle. Wright cites O.E. *on-tendan*, to kindle.

THAIVE, THEEVE.—A female sheep in its second year, before it has lambed.

THREAD OF LIFE.—The hanging plant "mother of thousands" (*Linaria cymbalaria*). So used at Ivinghoe. Wright explains it as "creeping saxifrage" (*Saxifraga sarmentosa*) in Northants.

TICKETY.—The wren (*Troglodytes parvulus*). (Beaconsfield.) Wright gives "ticky-tope" as used in Devon.

TIDDLY-BUMP.—As used in the phrase: "E come tiddly-bump down the batter." (I.)

TIFFLES.—Trifles.

TIGGLE.—To move slowly. "We was tigglin along tords . . ." (Very common in Bucks.)

TITTUP.—To walk lightly. "With his dog tittupping ahint him." (I.)

TODGE-BELLIED, TODGE-GUTTED.—Pot-bellied. Wright gives "tog-bellied" as obsolete in Gloucestershire, and "todd" as a disease in rabbits which causes a swelling of the stomach.

TOM AND JERRY.—A common beerhouse. (West Wycombe.)

TOM THUMB.—The lotus, or birdsfoot trefoil. (I.)

TUT.—Offence. "Take tut." (Winslow, rare.) Wright quotes Mr. Clear of Winslow for this; only authority.

TWIGGLY.—Twig-like. "You aint ought to it un wi that, but wi one of them thin little twiggly sticks." (I.)

TWIPPER.—To flicker. "Law! the lightnin just did twipper along it!" "They snipe be gallus ard to shoot; they do twipper and twirl about so." (I.)

UNKID.—Unpleasant, ugly, uncouth. Wright cites M.E. *unkid*, not made known; O.E. *cydan*, to make known.

'URK (*variant of* YARK).—Strap or piece of string to fasten trousers below the knee and keep them free from mud. (Gawcott and Wheeler End.)

WAD.—A bundle (of hay, cut corn, or straw).

WAG-WANTON.—Quaking grass (*Briza media*).

WAMBLY, WAMBLING.—Shaky on the legs. "A womblin ol os." (Wing.)

WANTEY.—The belly-band, used on cart-horses. The converse piece of harness is the ridget (*q.v.*). In general use and in sale catalogues. Wright cites O.E. *wamb*, belly, and *tige*, a band.

WATCHERD (*corruption of* WET-SHOD).—Wet-footed. Said to one who had walked through Grendon Underwood woods: "Then I'll warrnt as ees watcherd."

WATER-GOGGLES.—Marsh marigold (*Caltha palustris*). (Wing.)

WEST.—A sty in the eye. (Chesham.)

WHETILE.—The green woodpecker (*Gecinus viridis*). *Records of Bucks* (IX, 170) gives "wet dial" as the name of the wryneck at Chesham.

WHITE MONEY.—The plant alyssum. (Chesham.) Called "snow-in-harvest" at Ivinghoe.

WHITTLE.—To wear by friction. Said of a rope: "That'll whittle a-two." (Ford, Dinton.)

WIDBIN PEAR.—The white-beam tree (*Pyrus aria*). (West Wycombe.)

WIL-JILL (I.) WILLY-JOE (Ford, near Dinton). —An hermaphrodite. Not given by Wright. The derivation is an abbreviated form of William-Gillian.

WITHYWIND.—The lesser bindweed (*Convolvolus arvensis.*) Commonly used on the Chilterns, where it is an all too common weed. At Hambleden and Marlow it is called "bethwine." A more vigorous term for this weed is Devil's Guts.

WORLY.—Immoral, lascivious (of a man). (Downley and Gawcott.)

WUNG.—Preterite of "wing," to fling, hurt.

YAWNUPS.—A stupid person. (Gawcott.)

YELM.—Straw drawn out ready for the thatcher. (O.E. *gelm*, a handful, bundle.)

YOWE.—"Ewe," invariably so pronounced, rhyming with "slow."

APPENDIX

Method of Wichert Construction

In order to explain the term *berry*, or *bury*, it is desirable to give a particular account of the method of building wichert walls, especially as no such details are given in any book which deals with Buckinghamshire. The facts have kindly been furnished by Mr. Walter Rose, of Haddenham, and since he and his forbears have lived in that wichert-built village since the late sixteenth century, he may be allowed to be an authority on the subject.

A wall 14 to 16 inches thick, such as is made round a garden or orchard, is constructed in the following way: A foundation of rough stone is laid, the portion underground being wider than the thickness of the wall. Above the ground-level the stone, of the same thickness as the wall, is continued for a foot, and this portion is called the *grumpling*. By giving the wichert this kind of plinth, it is protected from the effects of rain splashing against it in wet weather.

Before this stone footing is made, the wichert (or whitchet), which is a kind of white marl found locally, is laid in heaps beside the line of the intended wall and well soaked with water. When the stonework is in position, the wichert is turned and short straw is trodden into it; the purpose of this is merely to keep it fairly compact whilst it is wet. The long, low heaps of wichert, lying parallel with the wall, are flattened out with the treading.

One man then stands on the stone grumpling and

165

holds the fork in front of him, with its tines resting on the grumpling. Another man with a similar fork digs a forkful of the wichert and smacks it down on the fork of the builder, who immediately turns it over and, with a smart pat, puts it in position. This process is repeated throughout the whole work of building the wall. The wichert is of the consistency of baker's dough and will keep its shape to the height of 2 feet or 2 feet 6 inches. As the berry reaches the required height, the builder walks backward slowly, until he reaches the end, where some kind of platform is made for him to stand upon.

One berry must be left to dry before another can be put on it, and the rate of drying depends on the season and weather. Three berries have been put on in a fortnight; at other times one berry may have to wait for that period or longer before it is fit to receive another on the top of it. When the berry is "about two-thirds dry," the sides are trimmed straight with a sharp spade, and each must be so trimmed before the next is put on it.

The lines of the berries can always be traced on an unplastered wall, and they never unite perfectly, since they always divide at these lines when a wall falls down.

Each berry is built thus, the builder standing on the dry one and walking backwards as he builds the next. When the height is greater than the man on the ground can pitch to, a third man is needed, who stands on a raised stage, also with a fork, taking the wichert from the first man and passing it to the builder. The walls of the Wesleyan and Baptist Chapels are built to the height of over 20 feet, and

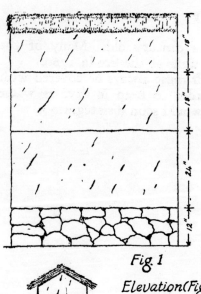

Fig. 1

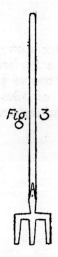

Fig. 3

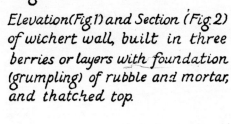

Fig. 2

Elevation(Fig.1) and Section (Fig.2) of wichert wall, built in three berries or layers with foundation (grumpling) of rubble and mortar, and thatched top.

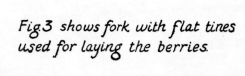

Fig.3 shows fork with flat tines used for laying the berries.

both are now over a century old. Many of the
village walls bear the signs of the fire in 1760.

The top of the wall must always be covered with
thatch or tiles in order to keep it dry, as water
standing on wichert would soon disintegrate it.